For Collectors Only®

Winchester Lever Action Repeating Firearms

Volume II

The Models of 1886 and 1892

by

Arthur Pirkle

North Cape Publications, Inc.®

THE MOSIN-NAGANT RIFLE

For my wife, **Patty**, who listened patiently for 40 years as I waxed rhapsodically on the euphoria attendant with collecting antiquities and lectured endlessly on the intricacies of Winchester originalities, all of which she undoubtedly found to be a monumental bore.

The author wishes to thank John Capalbo, John Edmondson and John Madl, CmfgE for their gracious assistance and advice in the preparation of this book.

Front cover: L-R: Montana Peak hat, circa 1895; rifle scabbard; reloading tool, .45-90; M1886 Carbine, Type 1 in .45-70; M1875 Cartridge Belt; .45-90 WCF Cartridges; M1892 Rifle (takedown) in .25-20 WCF; LF&C Hunting Knife; Skinning Knife in Buffalo Hide Sheath.

Copyright © 1996 and 2001 by North Cape Publications. All rights reserved. Reproduction or translations of any part of this work beyond that permitted by Section 107 or 108 of the 1976 United States Copyright Act without the written permission of the copyright holder is unlawful. Requests for permission or for further information should be addressed to the Permission Department, North Cape Publications.

This publication is designed to provide authoritative and accurate information in regard to the subject matter covered. However, it should be recognized that serial numbers and dates, as well as other information given within are necessarily limited by the accuracy of source materials.

ISBN 1-882391-13-6
North Cape Publications, Inc. P.O. Box 1027, Tustin, California 92781
Voice: 714 832-3621 **FAX**: 714 832-5302
Email: northcape@ix.netcom.com
Website: http://www.northcapepubs.com

Printed in USA by KNI, Inc., Anaheim, CA 92806

Table of Contents

CHAPTER 4 THE MODEL OF 1886 1
Conventions 8

BUTTPLATES 9
Buttplates—Rifles 9
Crescent-Style Buttplates 9
Shotgun-Style Buttplates 10
Buttplates—Carbines 11
Buttplate Screws 12

BUTTSTOCKS 13
Rifle Buttstock-Standard 13
Shotgun-Style Buttstocks for Rifles 17
Lightweight/Extra Lightweight Buttstocks 17
Pistol Grip Stocks 19
Pistol Grip Caps 19
Carbine Buttstocks 22
Rear Sling Swivel 22

RECEIVERS 25
Takedown Receiver Extension 27
Receiver—Finish 29
Upper Tang 30
Upper Tang Screws and Screw Holes 30
Model Markings 31
Lower Tang 33
Patent Markings 37
Serial Numbers 37
Assembly Numbers 38
Safety Catch 38
Pistol Grip Lower Tang 38
Hammers 39
Hammer Screw 40
Stirrup and Pin 41

Trigger/Sear 41
Trigger Spring and Screw 42
Finger Lever 42
Friction Stud Lever Catch 44
Friction Stud Spring and Pin 44
Saddle Ring and Stud 44
Breechbolts 45
Finger Lever/Breechbolt Pin 47
Extractor Pin 48
Firing Pin Stop Pin 48
Locking Bolts 48
Extractor 50
Ejector 50

SPRINGS 52
Mainspring 52
Carrier Spring and Screw 52

ACTION 54
Carrier 54
Carrier Hook 55
Cartridge Guide 56
Cartridge Stop 56
Loading Gate Assembly 57
Loading Gate Base 58
Loading Gate Leaf 58
Loading Gate Spring 58
Loading Gate Pin 59
Loading Gate Screw 59
Loading Gate Stop Pin 59
Firing Pins 59

FORENDS AND FOREARMS 61
Rifle Forends 61
Carbine Forearms 62
Rifle Forend Tips 64
Carbine Forearm Tips 65

Forend Tip Tenon 66
Forend Tip Screws 67

BARRELS 68
Barrel Crown 72
Dovetails 72
Barrel Markings 74
Barrel Address Markings—Rifle 74
Barrel Address Markings-Carbine 75
Nickel Steel Barrel Markings 76
Winchester Proof Mark 77
Caliber Markings 77
Other Markings 78
The Problem of Barrel Changes 78
Rear Barrel Bands 79
Rear Barrel Band Spring 80
Rear Barrel Band Screw 80
Sling Hooks or Eyes 80
Front Barrel Band—Carbine 82
Front Barrel Band Screw 82

MAGAZINE TUBES 83
Magazine End Plugs For Non-Takedown Rifles and Carbines 85
Magazine End Plug Screws 87
Magazine Followers 88
Magazine Spring 88
Takedown Magazine End Plugs 89
Takedown Magazine Takedown Levers 90
Magazine Plunger and Spring 91
Magazine Tube Ring 91
Magazine Tube Ring Pin 93

REAR SIGHTS 93
Rifle Rear Sights 93
Carbine Rear Sights 95
Special Order Rear Sights 96
Front Sights 97

Rifle Front Sights 97
Carbine Front Sights 98

M1886 SCREW TYPES AND SIZES 99

CHAPTER 5 THE MODEL OF 1892 103
BUTTPLATES 105
Buttplates—Rifle 106
Buttplates—Carbines 107
Buttplates—Color Case-Hardened 110
Buttplate Screws 110
Buttstocks 111
Buttstocks—Rifle 111
Buttstocks—Carbine 112
"Eastern Carbines" 114
Gumwood Stocks 115
Pistol Grip Stocks 115
Sling Swivels 116
Rear Sling Swivel 116

RECEIVERS 118
Serial Numbers 119
Dimensions 121
Takedown Extension 121
Upper Tang 123
Upper Tang Markings 124
Other Upper Tang Markings 128
Lower Tang 128
Trigger/Sear 130
Trigger Pin 131
Hammer 131
Hammer Screw 133
Stirrup and Pin 133

ACTION 134
Carrier and Carrier Screws 134
Cartridge Guides, Screws and Stops 135

vi

Left Cartridge Guide—.25 and .32 Calibers, Type 1 135
Left Cartridge Guide—.38 and .44 Calibers, Type 2 137
Right Cartridge Guides 138
Cartridge Stop 138
Cartridge Guide Screws 139
Saddle Rings 140

BREECHBOLTS 141
Locking Bolts 144
Locking Bolt Pin 145
Locking Bolt Pin Stop Screw 146
Extractor 146
Ejector Assembly 147
Firing Pin 148
Finger Lever 148
Friction Stud, Spring and Stop Pin 149
Loading Gate 150
Mainspring 150
Trigger Spring 152
Cartridge Stop Spring 152

FORENDS AND FOREARMS 153
Trapper or Baby Carbine Forearms 153
Forend Tips 154
Type 3 Forend Tips for "Button Magazine" Rifles 156
Forend Tip Tenon 157

BARRELS 158
Barrel Rifling 159
Barrel Crowns 160
Dovetails 160
Barrel Markings 162
Caliber Markings 165
Barrel Markings—Trapper/Baby Carbines 165
Barrel Proof Mark 166
Stainless Steel Barrels 166
Barrel Bands 167

Front Barrel Bands 167
Rear Barrel Bands 167
Barrel Band Screws 168
Front Sling Eye 169
Magazine Tubes 170
Magazine Tube End Plugs 172
Magazine Follower 174
Magazine End Plug Screws 174
Magazine Tube Spring 175
Magazine Tube Rings 176

SIGHTS 178
Rifle Rear Sight 178
Carbine Rear Sight 180
Front Sights 180
Rifle Front Sight 180
Carbine Front Sights 181
Special Order Sights 182
Tang Sight 182
Side-Mounted Receiver Rear Sight 183
M1892 Screw Types and Sizes 183

APPENDIX A: M1886 SERIAL NUMBERS 186
APPENDIX B: M1892 SERIAL NUMBERS 188
APPENDIX C: SPECIAL ORDER BARRELS 190
APPENDIX D: THE MODEL 1886 .50 CALIBER RIFLE AND CARBINE ... 192
APPENDIX E: GUIDE TO WINCHESTER AMMUNITION 194
APPENDIX F: GLOSSARY 196
APPENDIX G: BIBLIOGRAPHY 200
APPENDIX H: THE CODY FIREARMS MUSEUM, BUFFALO BILL HISTORICAL
    CENTER 202
ABOUT THE AUTHOR 202

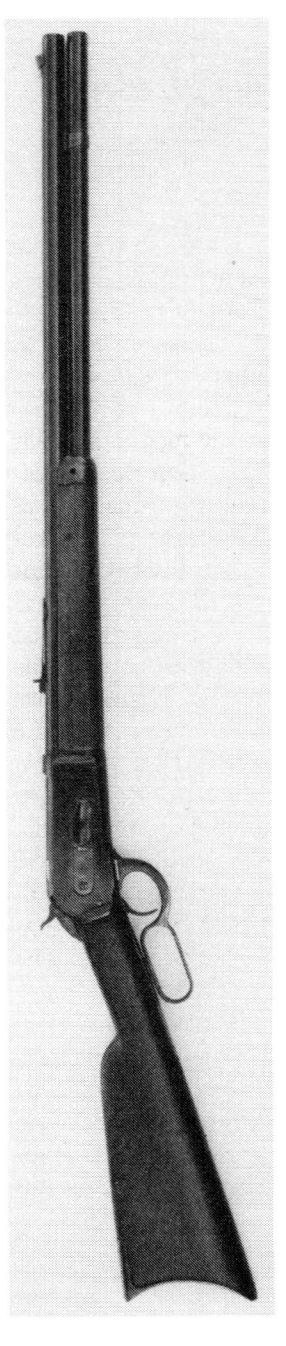

Model 1886 rifle from the collection of Ed Koenig, fully restored by Dave Fessenden, Restoration Resource (Georgetown, CO) and Custom Gunsmith and Engraving (Blackhawk, SD). Photography by Bill Hotchkiss. Only original parts were used in the restoration and original finishes were preserved or duplicated.

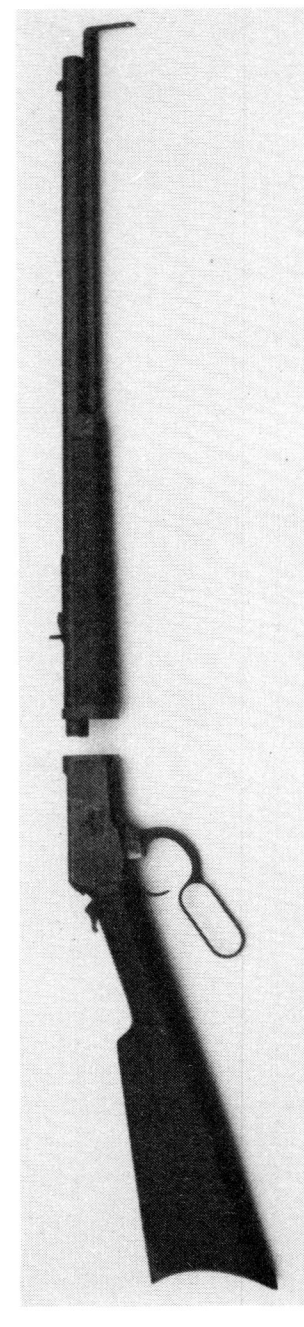

Model 1892 Rifle, takedown variation, in .25-30 caliber. From the collection of John Capalbo.

Winchester Lever Action Repeating Firearms
The Models of 1886 and 1892
Volume II

This is the second in a three volume series which will describe the complete range of Winchester Lever Action Repeating rifles, carbines and muskets. As in previous books in the **For Collectors Only®** series, each part will be examined individually and described in terms of material, finish, markings and other identifying characteristics by serial number range.

In this volume, the fourth and fifth repeating models to bear the Winchester name, the Models 1886 and 1892, are described. Volume III will include the Models 1894 and 1895, and Volume IV will describe the continuation Models 71, 53, 65, 55 and 64, the musket versions of previous models and instructions for disassembly, repair and reassembly of the Winchester lever action repeating family.

Identifying and quantifying Winchester Lever Action Repeating arms is complicated by the fact that Winchester often used parts of the same or similar design for a number of different models. i.e., rifle buttplates used for the Models 1892, 1894 and 1895 will interchange, while the Model 1886 rifle buttplate is the same configuration but is slightly larger.

Serial numbers for the M1886 and M1892 are included in Appendices A and B. Appendix C describes special order barrels, Appendix D contains a point-by-point identification guide to the .50 Caliber Model 1886 Rifle and carbine. Appendix E describes all commercial ammunition produced for the M1886 and M1892 rifle, Appendix F contains a glossary and Appendix G, the Bibliography. The final Appendix, H, describes the procedure for obtaining a "factory" letter from the Cody Firearms Museum, Buffalo Bill Historical Center at Cody, Wyoming, the official repository of Winchester records.

This series deals only with standard production rifles, carbines and muskets. The collector should keep in mind however, that all engraved and other special order guns were built on standard receivers and parts before being embellished. When exceptions occur to this rule, they are noted in the text.

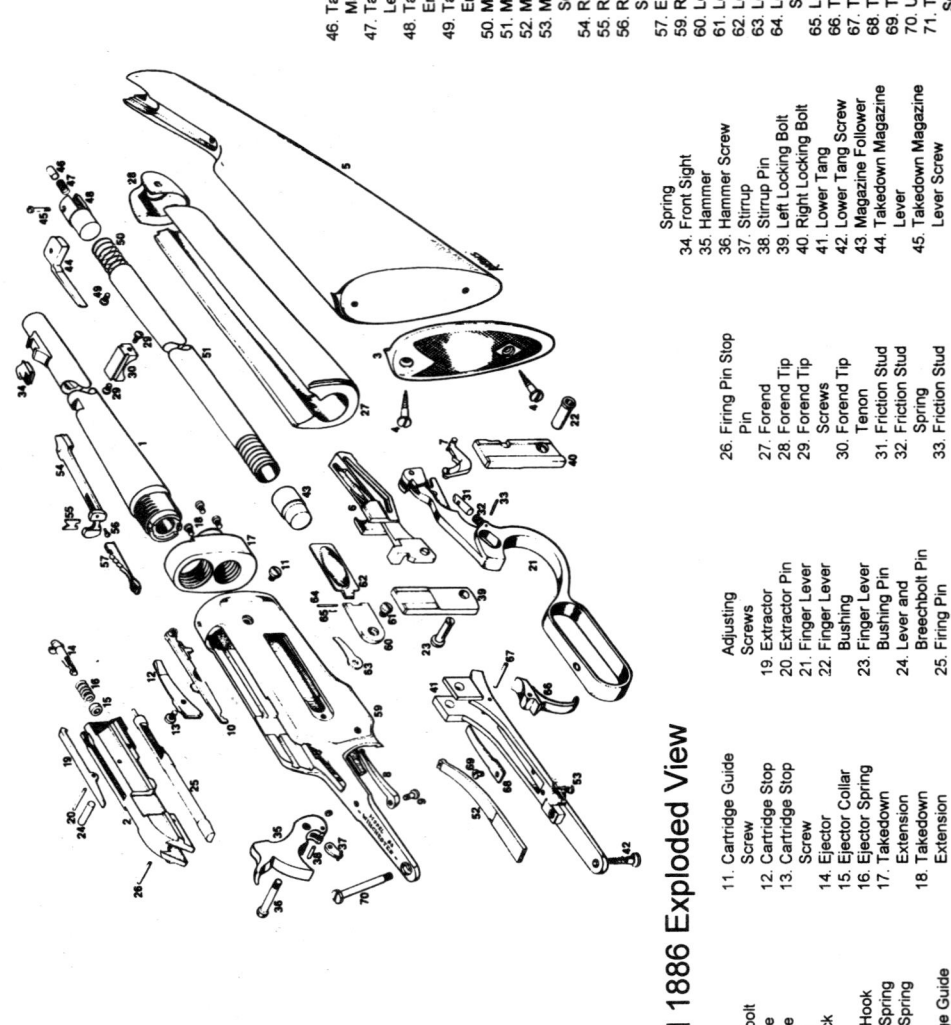

Model 1886 Exploded View

1. Barrel
2. Breechbolt
3. Buttplate
4. Buttplate Screws
5. Buttstock
6. Carrier
7. Carrier Hook
8. Carrier Spring
9. Carrier Spring Screw
10. Cartridge Guide
11. Cartridge Guide Screw
12. Cartridge Stop
13. Cartridge Stop Screw
14. Ejector
15. Ejector Collar
16. Ejector Spring
17. Takedown Extension
18. Takedown Extension
19. Extractor
20. Extractor Pin
21. Finger Lever
22. Finger Lever Bushing
23. Finger Lever Bushing Pin
24. Lever and Breechbolt Pin
25. Firing Pin
26. Firing Pin Stop Pin
27. Forend
28. Forend Tip
29. Forend Tip Screws
30. Forend Tip Tenon
31. Friction Stud
32. Friction Stud Spring
33. Friction Stud
34. Front Sight
35. Hammer
36. Hammer Screw
37. Stirrup
38. Stirrup Pin
39. Left Locking Bolt
40. Right Locking Bolt
41. Lower Tang
42. Lower Tang Screw
43. Magazine Follower
44. Takedown Magazine Lever
45. Takedown Magazine Lever Screw
46. Takedown Magazine Plunger
47. Takedown Magazine Lever Spring
48. Takedown Magazine End Plug
49. Takedown Magazine End Plug Screw
50. Magazine Spring
51. Magazine Tube
52. Mainspring
53. Mainspring Strain Screw
54. Rear Sight
55. Rear Sight Blade
56. Rear Sight Blade Screw
57. Elevator
59. Receiver
60. Loading Gate Base
61. Loading Gate Screw
62. Loading Gate Leaf
63. Loading Gate Spring
64. Leaf Spring Retaining Spring
65. Loading Gate Stop Pin
66. Trigger/Sear
67. Trigger Pin
68. Trigger Spring
69. Trigger Spring Screw
70. Upper Tang Screw
71. Tang Sight Plug Screw

Spring

The Models of 1886 and 1892

WINCHESTER LEVER ACTION REPEATERS, VOLUME 2, THE MODELS 1886 AND 1892

CHAPTER 4 THE MODEL OF 1886

The Model 1886 was Winchester's first repeating rifle designed by the firearms genius, John Moses Browning. After the failure of the Model 1876 to safely fire the 45-70 Government cartridge with a 405 or 500 grain bullet, the company asked Mr. Browning to design a rifle that would. The Model 1886 was basically a large M1892, another very popular gun that Mr. Browning designed for Winchester. The M1886 with its double vertical locking bolt action was, in addition to being very strong, a radical departure from Winchester's old tried and true toggle link system as employed in its three previous repeating models. The basic Henry rifle toggle link system in those models previous to the M1886 had been the sole system employed by Winchester in their lever action repeaters since Oliver Winchester purchased the Henry Rifle Company some twenty years previously.

A total of 156,599 Model 1886 arms were made in ten *production* calibers between 1886 and 1935 when production was discontinued. The emphasis on the word "production" is necessary inasmuch as the M1886, according to existing factory records housed in the Buffalo Bill Historical Center's firearms museum at Cody, Wyoming, indicates this model was actually manufactured in a total of 43 distinctly different calibers, albeit many of them experimental and of very limited production—quite often only one. Production records list 134,299 rifles, 6,223 carbines and 374 muskets as having been manufactured. The reason for the disparity between the above figures and the total number of arms produced as given in the first sentence of this paragraph is that data pertaining to approximately 15,000 arms were either never recorded or have been lost. No data at all were entered in the Model 1886 ledgers from serial number 146,000 to serial number 150,799—a total of 4,799 arms. The Winchester Model 71 was a

Winchester Lever Action Repeaters

modernized version of the Model 1886, produced from 1936 to 1958. Of the Model 1886 arms for which records are available to the researcher, the following table has been compiled.

TABLE 4-1
MODEL 1886 WINCHESTER VARIATIONS

VARIATION	NUMBER	% OF PRODUCTION
Rifle	134,295	95.3
Carbine	6,223	4.4
Musket	374	0.37
TRIGGERS		
TYPE	NUMBER	% OF PRODUCTION
Plain	132,055	94.0
Set	8,486	6.0
MAGAZINES		
TYPE	NUMBER	% OF PRODUCTION
Full	125,091	80
Half	15,539	10
2/3	240	0.2
3/4	169	0.1
STOCKS		
VARIATION	NUMBER	% OF PRODUCTION
Straight grip	129,579	91.9
Pistol grip	6,407	4.5
Checkered	5,014	3.6

The Models of 1886 and 1892

Variation	Number	% of Production
Barrels		
Variation	Number	% of production
Round	45,693	32.5
Octagon	91,862	65.3
Half round/half octagon	3,131	2.2
Barrel Length (inches)		
Length	Number	% of production
14	1	Infinitesimal (Inf.)
14.5	498	0.4 (line throwing guns)
20	113	0.1
21	5	Inf.
22	8,436	6.0
22.5	1	Inf.
23	1	Inf.
24	1,304	0.9
25	5	Inf.
26	122,770	87.1
27	7	Inf.
28	5,068	3.6
29	33	Inf.

Winchester Lever Action Repeaters

Variation	Number	% of Production
30	1,874	1.4
31	1	Inf.
32	574	0.4
33	7	Inf.
34	35	Inf.
36	60	Inf.
38	2	Inf.

Calibers

Caliber	Number	% of production
.22	2	Inf.
.22 Long	1	Inf.
.22-86	1	Inf.
.30	3	Inf.
.310 Bore	1	Inf.
.31-62	2	Inf.
.32	4	Inf.
.33*	12,457	8.9
.38-50	1	Inf.
.38-51	1	Inf.
.38-53	1	Inf.
.38-55	6	Inf.

The Models of 1886 and 1892

Variation	Number	% of Production
.38-56*	18,483	13.2
.38-70*	830	0.6
.38-72	1	Inf.
.40 Express	1	Inf.
.40-33	1	Inf.
.40-60	1	Inf.
.40-61	1	Inf.
.40-65*	16,315	11.6
.40-70*	629	0.4
.40-72	1	Inf.
.40-80	2	Inf.
.40-82*	29,646	21.1
.40-85	5	Inf.
.40-95	1	Inf.
.44	9	Inf.
.45	1	Inf.
.45-50	1	Inf.
.45-60	1	Inf.
.45-70*	34,859	24.9
.45-72	4	Inf.
.45-75	5	Inf.

Winchester Lever Action Repeaters

VARIATION	NUMBER	% OF PRODUCTION
.45-80	1	Inf.
.45-90*	21,553	15.4
.45-92	2	Inf.
.46	1	Inf.
.50-100	1	Inf.
.50-100-450*	234	0.2
.50-105	15	Inf.
.50-110*	5,046	3.6
.86-50 Express	1	Inf.
* Standard production caliber		

It should be noted that the approximate 15,000 arms records for the M1886 that are lost, if found, would change these statistics significantly. The collector should also note that some calibers listed could be simple clerical errors. The .22-86 and the .86-50 caliber guns are particularly suspect. A caliber .95-30 arm is listed in the Model 1895 ledger, but this also could be a clerical error.

The author discovered while researching factory records at the Cody Firearms Museum that on occasions when Winchester's regular record's clerk was absent from work, his temporary replacement(s) may have added to the confusion by entering data pertaining to other models. Several instances of information for the Model 1885 Single Shot Rifle with octagon barrels in .32-40 caliber appear in the M1886 records. Upon checking the ledger for the Model 1885, no listing was found for those serial numbers at all. These entries were in a handwriting quite different from that throughout the other pages in this section of the ledger.

The Models of 1886 and 1892

There are also notes in these records indicating that 188 receivers (only) were produced. It is logical to assume that at least some and possibly all of these were never assembled into complete arms. If true, this could also alter the numbers listed for a particular caliber.

The issue is further clouded by the fact that there are also several notes in these same records indicating that two guns, quite often in different calibers, were produced and marked with the same serial number. An exception: the unique .310 bore gun was actually produced as a complete firearm, was subsequently marked as "experimental," and is now on display at Cody.

The Barrel Length section of Table 4-1 indicates that 8,436 arms were produced with the standard carbine length 22 inch barrel while the Type of Arms section indicates only 6,223 carbines were made. This, of course, means that a total of 2,213 rifles were made in what modern collectors refer to as the "short-rifle" configuration.

Of interest to the collector and researcher alike is the puzzling fact that the first .38-70 caliber arm was manufactured at circa serial #18,000, while the next gun in this very rare caliber does not occur until circa serial #85,000, when the even more rarely encountered caliber 40-70 arms first begin to appear.

Of major importance to the collector are the "heavy" and "extra heavy" and "lightweight" and "extra lightweight" barrels. These special order guns command a significant premium, which in turn, requires that the collector examine any Winchester lever action with such a barrel with the utmost care. These premium barrels are discussed in detail both in the barrel section and in Appendix C.

Caliber commands a premium with modern collectors of the M1886, probably more so than with any other model. The most desirable caliber is the .50-Express (.50-100, .50-105, .50-110) followed by the .45-90 and .45-70 in that order. Following, are the somewhat less desirable calibers of .40-82, .38-56, .40-65, and .33 Winchester in that order. The .40-70 and .38-70 caliber guns are extremely rare and very seldom encountered, but strangely enough, do not command a premium. Models 1886 in the extremely rare .50-100 caliber, al-

Winchester Lever Action Repeaters

though they are known to exist, are really the .50-110 caliber with a different bullet weight and powder loading. As rare as M1886s are in this caliber, a rifle or carbine so chambered would presumably command a premium even over the 50-110 caliber counterpart. Bear in mind that the popularity of these premium calibers are with the modern collector only. The 19th and early 20th Century purchaser of the M1886 always preferred the ten calibers marked with an asterisk in Table 4-1.

Conventions

1. "Standard" refers to rifles, carbines and muskets that were not ordered with "special" features. 2. "Right side" or "left side" refers to the side of the firearm to the shooter's right or left when shouldered properly. 3. All directions are given from the shooter's point of view—i.e., looking toward the muzzle. 4. All references are to Winchester *lever action repeating* firearms only. 5. All changes in parts are shown occurring "circa" a given serial number. Most changes were introduced gradually during production and as many as several thousand firearms could have been built before the transition from one part to another was completed. Exceptions are noted. 6) Quotation marks are often used in the text to indicate factory-applied markings. The quotation marks were not part of the factory-applied marking unless noted otherwise. 7) Screw hole measurements are from the point used as an index to the center of the hole, unless otherwise stated. 8) The reader may find information repeated several times throughout the text. This has been done deliberately to save having to turn back and forth to find specific information. 9) If you are uncertain of the definition of a specific term used in the text, refer to the glossary in Appendix F.

The Models of 1886 and 1892

BUTTPLATES

Buttplates—Rifles

Two types of buttplates were installed on the M1886 rifle. The **Type 1** was a crescent-style steel buttplate. At circa serial #96,000, the **Type 2** shotgun-style steel or hard rubber buttplate was introduced. It predominated toward the end of production and was also used on the M71.

Crescent-Style Buttplates

M1886 rifle buttplates to circa serial #95,000 were nearly identical to those used on the Model 1876 even to the forward protruding toe at the bottom. They were *never* made with the trap door for access to a butt trap storage compartment, except on special order.

NOTE: Most parts breakdowns and assembly guides show the M1886 buttplate with the trapdoor installed, but they were only incorporated on special order, and then rarely. If a M1886 has a trapdoor buttplate, it was probably removed from a M1876 rifle. Only a factory letter can assure authenticity. See Appendix H.

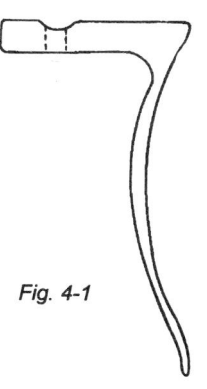

Fig. 4-1

Two variations of crescent-style rifle buttplates were used on the M1886 rifle. The **Type 1A** was installed to circa serial #60,000 and appears similar to those used on the M1892 and M1894, except for their considerably larger size. The overall dimensions were 4 3/8 inches long by 1 3/8 inches wide at the widest point. The upper tang was 2 9/32-2 11/32 inches long. See Figure 4-1.

The Type 1A crescent buttplate is identifiable by the forward protruding toe, 3/8 ± 1/64 inches long, also installed on the early M1876 rifles.

The switch from the Type 1A to the **Type 1B** crescent buttplate took place over a long transition period starting at circa serial #60,000 and

Winchester Lever Action Repeaters

ending at circa serial #95,000, after which the Type 1B was installed exclusively. The Type 1B crescent buttplate upper tang was reduced in size to 1 9/16-1 19/32 inches long. See Figure 4-2.

Fig. 4-2

NOTE: Early rifles with Type 1B Crescent buttplates were "special order" rifles. Winchester apparently allowed individual assemblers to use up their supply of the long-tang buttplates before switching to the short tang. It also appears as if the special-order shop ran out of the Type 1A buttplates before the assemblers did.

Model 1886 steel buttplates were color case hardened to circa serial #115,000. Between circa serial #115,000 and circa serial #130,000, a gradual transition was made to a blued finish. Color case hardening of any M1886 part, including the buttplate, continued to be available on a special order basis until production ended in 1932. Many "special order" M1886s were produced with no other feature than color case hardening.

Shotgun-Style Buttplates

After circa serial #95,000, and including most Model 71 .348 caliber rifles, the **Type 2** shotgun-style buttplate was installed concurrently with the Type 1B. See Figure 4-3. Four variations were used:

Type 2A: steel checkered metal buttplate similar to those used on pre-1964 Model 70s. It had a short 1/4 inch tang that tapered to a sharp front edge.

Type 2B: smooth steel buttplates as used on special order Model 1876 rifles equipped with the shotgun butt. It had a short 1/4 inch tang that tapered to a sharp front edge.

Fig. 4-3

Type 2C: hard rubber shotgun-style buttplate with a short 1/4 inch tang that tapered to a sharp front edge.

The Models of 1886 and 1892

Type 2D: hard rubber buttplate without a spur or tang at the top. These were installed on many "Extra Lightweight" M1886 rifle variations .

Buttplates—Carbines

Carbine buttplates were similar to those used on the M1892 and M1894 carbines, but were larger in all dimensions. M1886 carbine buttplates were 4 5/32 to 4 7/32 inches long and 1 15/32 ± 1/32 inches wide. The tang was 1 15/16 ± 1/32 inches long, 1 3/32 inches wide at the rear and 9/16 inches wide at the front. They were 3/32 inches thick at the edges. See Figure 4-4.

Standard carbine buttplates, like their rifle counterparts, did not have the trap door for access to a cleaning rod compartment.

Fig. 4-4

M1886 carbine buttplates had a milled-out portion 3 9/16 inches long by 23/32 inches wide and 1/16 inches deep on the inside surface of the plate. The upper edge of this milled-out portion was cut straight across at right angles to the height of the plate while the lower edge was rounded at the toe with the result that the edge was 1/16 inch thicker than the rest of the base, 13/64 inches wide at its narrowest point and 3/8 inches at the widest. This milled-out section was apparently an attempt by Winchester to reduce the weight of the M1886 carbine. See Figure 4-5.

NOTE: M1892 and M1894, as well as all reproduction carbine buttplates, lack this milled-out interior which makes this an excellent way to determine if a M1886 carbine buttplate is original.

Fig. 4-5

Winchester Lever Action Repeaters

A very few carbines were "special ordered" with shotgun butts. These were extremely rare and are almost never seen today outside private collections. Any M1886 carbine with a shotgun-style buttplate should be examined carefully. Wood to metal fit should be perfect with the wood "proud." If the buttstock does not fit well around the tangs and the receiver but the buttplate fits the butt-area of the stock properly, it may be a rifle buttstock installed after the carbine left the factory. There were relatively few M1886 carbines made, they saw hard use and their survival rate was minimal. Therefore, original replacement stocks are almost impossible to find.

Buttplate Screws

The buttplate screws for the Model 1886 were interchangeble with those used on all other models. They were oval-head wood screws with beveled shoulders 1 17/64 inches long. The head was 11/32 inches in diameter, the shank was 1 11/64 inches long by 7/32 inches in diameter and was threaded from the bottom 7/8 inches of its length. See Figure 4-6.

Fig. 4-6

The Models of 1886 and 1892

BUTTSTOCKS

Buttstocks for the M1886 Winchester were made of straight-grained American walnut, although a variety of other woods and grain patterns were also available on special order. The standard stock had a straight wrist but pistol grip stocks were also available on special order.

Until 1895, Winchester used two different sized blanks for their lever action buttstocks, the larger for the M1876 and M1886, the smaller for the M1866, M1873, M1892, M1894 and M1895. Both sizes had the long lower tang groove, the long buttplate upper tang cutout and the forward pointing buttplate toe. In that year, Winchester decided to simplify their inventory and changed from the larger to a smaller buttstock for the M1886 which was almost indistinguishable from those installed on the M1892, M1894 and M1895.

The M1886 buttstock can be differentiated from the M1876 by its shorter lower tang cutout which was 43/64 inches wide at the front, 33/64 inches wide at the rear by 5 21/32 $\pm$ 1/64 inches long. The M1886 lower tang cut is therefore slightly shorter than the lower tang cut on the M1876 (5 3/4 inches long) stock, but longer than that on the M1866, M1873, M1892, M1894 and M1895. The M1886 lower tang cut is also wider than the M1876 tang cut (35/64 at the front and 1/2 inches at the rear).

Rifle Buttstock-Standard

M1886 rifles were not drilled for a cleaning rod compartment in the buttstock except on special order. The M1886 rifle buttstocks did have a "hole" 4 1/4 inches deep by 45/64 inches in diameter, too short for the four section cleaning rod. It was drilled only to mount the stock blank on the milling machine.

Any cleaning rod compartments cut on special order would have been 45/64 inches in diameter by 7 9/16 inches deep. A buttplate with a trap door, spring and screw would have also been installed.

Winchester Lever Action Repeaters

NOTE: The M1886 rifle was sold with a slotted hickory cleaning rod 9/32 inches in diameter and 30 inches long, far too long to fit in the 4 1/4 inch deep mounting hole in the buttstock.

The **Type 1** M1886 standard rifle buttstock (See Figure 4-7) was shaped for the crescent buttplate and used to between circa serial #60,000-95,000. Its measurements are shown in Table 4-2.

The Type 1 rifle buttstocks for the crescent buttplate to between circa serial #60,000-95,000 were almost indistinguishable from those installed on the M1876. The M1876 had a slightly longer lower tang (5 3/4 inches vs. 5 21/32 inches long) and its mainspring stud was mounted 1/4 inches farther to the rear than on the M1886.

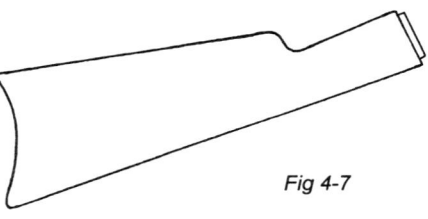

Fig 4-7

The extreme rear of the M1886 lower tang was more sharply pointed than the M1876. The stocks were therefore not interchangeable without major modifications to the lower tang cutout which will generally reveal itself on close examination. See page 33 for lower tang dimensions. Between circa serial #60-000-95,000, the **Type 2** M1886 standard rifle buttstock (See Figure 4-8) shaped for the crescent buttplate was cut smaller when Winchester standardized sizes. Type 2 buttstock measurements are listed in Table 4-3.

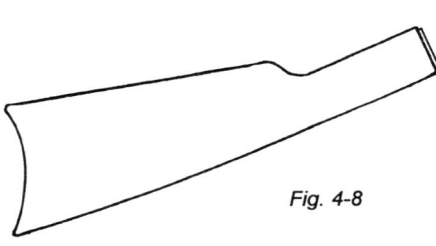

Fig. 4-8

NOTE: Type 2 buttstocks will replace Type 1 buttstocks on the receiver and vice versa, but their buttplates will not interchange.

The Models of 1886 and 1892

Area Measured	Measurement (inches)
\multicolumn{2}{c}{**Table 4-2**}

Area Measured	Measurement (inches)
Length across bottom (front to toe) less lip	14 3/8
Length across top (front to heel) less lip	12 3/4
Height at front of comb	2 37/64
Height, center of wrist	1 39/64
Width, center of wrist	1 7/16
Height at front of buttplate tang cutout	4 5/16
Height at extreme rear of buttstock	4 1/32
Width at extreme rear of buttstock	1 15/32
Width at center bulge	1 17/32
Upper Tang Grove: Length Width	3 3/4 29/32 (front) 17/32 (rear)
Lower Tang Groove: Length Width	5 21/32 43/64 (front) 33/64 (rear)

Buttplate Screw Holes; Distance from top to center of hole:
    Top Screw
    Bottom Screw
	1/2 inch from front edge of buttplate tang cutout
	1 11/32 above point of toe

Table 4-2
M1886 Rifle Buttstock Measurements
Circa Serial #1-60,000 to 95,000
(Accuracy ± 1/32 to 1/4 inches)*

* Expected variation in actual measurements from those listed due to manufacturing tolerances and shrinking and drying of aged wood.

Winchester Lever Action Repeaters

TABLE 4-3
M1886 RIFLE BUTTSTOCK MEASUREMENTS
CIRCA SERIAL #95,000 TO END OF PRODUCTION
(ACCURACY ± 1/32 TO 1/4 INCHES)*

AREA MEASURED	MEASUREMENT (INCHES)
Length across bottom (front to toe) less lip	14 1/8
Length across top (front to heel) less lip	12 3/4
Height at center of comb	3 1/4
Height, center of wrist	1 35/64
Width, center of wrist	1 19/64
Height at front of buttplate tang cutout	3 1/2
Height at extreme rear of buttstock	3 39/64
Height at rear, forward of buttplate cutout	3 51/64
Width at extreme rear of buttstock	1 7/16
Width at center bulge	1 25/64

Upper Tang Grove:
    Length
    Width
	3 3/4
	29/32 (front) 17/32 (rear)

Lower Tang Groove:
    Length
    Width
	5 3/8
	43/64 (front) 33/64 (rear)

Buttplate Screw Holes; Distance from top to center of hole:
    Top Screw
    Bottom Screw
	7/16 inch to rear of front edge of buttplate tang cutout
	1 7/16 above point of toe

* Expected variation in actual measurements from those listed due to manufacturing tolerances and shrinking and drying of aged wood.

The Models of 1886 and 1892

Shotgun-Style Buttstocks for Rifles
Two types of Shotgun-style buttstocks were installed on the M1886 rifle on special order. See Figure 4-9. To circa serial #145,000, the **Type 1** Shotgun-style stock had a 5/16 inches deep cutout for the spur or tang on the Type 2 metal shotgun buttplate or Type 3 hard rubber buttplate. After, the **Type 2** Shotgun-style stock omitted the 5/16 inch cutout and was fitted with the Type 4 hard rubber buttplate which lacked the spur.

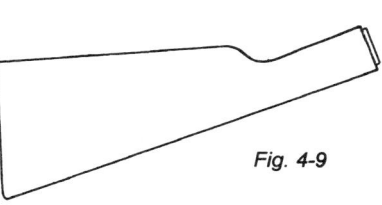

Fig. 4-9

Special order guns with shotgun butts to circa serial #145,000 were almost always the Type 1 with the spur. After, they were seen less frequently until they disappeared near the end of the M1886 production run.

Shotgun-style buttstocks were always installed on lightweight and extra-lightweight rifles.

The measurements for the shotgun buttstock are given in Table 4-4.

Lightweight/Extra Lightweight Buttstocks
At circa serial #115,000, Winchester introduced the "Lightweight" and "Extra Lightweight" M1886 rifle variations. To reduce their weight as much as possible, an oval-shaped cutout 2 5/32 inches high by 41/64 inches wide and tapering to a relatively sharp point after 6 inches was made in the rear of the buttstock. The cutout did reduce the weight but also moved the center of gravity farther toward the muzzle and left the M1886 still heavier than its competition. See Figure 4-10.

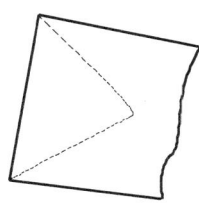

Fig. 4-10

Winchester Lever Action Repeaters

TABLE 4-4
M1886 RIFLE SHOTGUN BUTTSTOCK MEASUREMENTS
(ACCURACY ± 1/32 TO 1/4 INCHES)*

AREA MEASURED	MEASUREMENT (INCHES)
Length across bottom (front to toe) less lip	13 3/4
Length across top (front to heel) less lip	12 11/64
Width at front of comb	1 13/32
Width at front of grip	1 13/32
Height at extreme rear of buttstock	5 1/16
Width at extreme rear of buttstock	1 5/8
Length of Buttplate tang cutout **	5/16

Upper Tang Groove:
    Length
    Width
	3 3/4
	29/32 (front) 17/32 (rear)

Lower Tang Groove:
    Length
    Width
	5 3/8
	43/64 (front) 33/64 (rear)

Buttplate Screw Holes, Distance from top to center of hole:
    Top Screw
    Bottom Screw
	
	7/16
	3 3/4

*   Expected variation in actual measurements from those listed due to manufacturing tolerances and shrinking and drying of aged wood.

** The majority of early "Extra Lightweight" rifles were equipped with the hard rubber buttplate which had a pointed spur or tang to circa serial #145,000. After, they were made without the spur and the cut on the stock was eliminated.

The Models of 1886 and 1892

The Type 2 shotgun-style buttplate was always fitted to these special order rifles. The lightweight rifle received the Type 2A steel shotgun-style buttplate; the extra-lightweight rifle received the Type 2C or Type 2D shotgun-style buttplate.

Pistol Grip Stocks

Pistol grip stocks were fairly common on the M1886 rifle, but extremely rare on carbines. Almost all pistol grip variations of the Model 1886 will show burl grain in the buttstock and usually in the forearm as well, unless the customer specifically stated otherwise. Special order guns in this model were fitted with what Winchester referred to then as "special finish" wood.

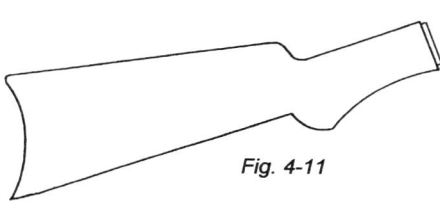

Fig. 4-11

There are known original M1886 rifles equipped with straight grain walnut pistol grip buttstocks, although quite rare and almost always seen toward the end of production when the Type 2 buttstocks were standard. See Figures 4-11 and 4-12 and Table 4-5.

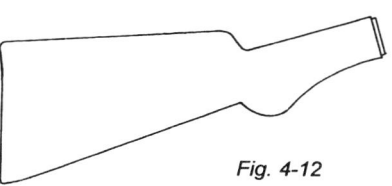

Fig. 4-12

Pistol Grip Caps

The pistol grips were finished in one of two ways. The **Type 1** was an ebony inlay, form-fitted and set into the wood itself. It was used to circa serial #90,000 and was similar to those used on the M1873 and M1876. Strictly speaking it was not a cap.

After circa serial #90,000, the **Type 2** pistol grip cap was made of hard rubber. It had the Winchester logo impressed in a circular pattern into its outer edge.

Winchester Lever Action Repeaters

TABLE 4-5
M1886 RIFLE PISTOL GRIP BUTTSTOCK MEASUREMENTS
(ACCURACY ± 1/32 TO 1/4 INCHES)*

AREA MEASURED	MEASUREMENT (INCHES)
Length across bottom (front to toe) less lip	14 7/16 ± 3/32 crescent buttplate 13 15/16 ± 3/32 shotgun butt
Length across top (front to heel) less lip	13 ± 3/32 crescent butt plate 12 3/4 ± 3/32 shotgun butt
Width at front of comb	1 23/64 ± 1/16
Width at front of grip	1 25/64 ± 1/32
Height at extreme rear of buttstock	3 3/4 ± 1/16 crescent buttplate 5 1/32 ± 3/32 shotgun butt
Width at extreme rear of buttstock	1 5/16 ± 1/16 crescent buttplate 1 37/64 ± 1/32 shotgun butt
Length of Buttplate tang cutout **	1 5/64 tang cutout, crescent buttplate 5/16 ± 1/32 spur cutout, shotgun butt
Upper Tang Groove: Length Width	3 27/32 ± 1/32 29/32 (rear) 1/2 ± 1/64 (rear)
Lower Tang Groove: Length Width	3 3/4 43/64 ± 1/64 (front) 37/64 ± 1/64 (rear)

ButtplateScrewHoles:
Crescent: Top Screw
                      Bottom Screw
Shotgun: Top Screw
                      Bottom Screw
	
	7/16 inch from forward edge of tang cutout to center of hole
	1 7/16 above point of toe
	9/32
	1 1/4

*   Variations may be due to wood shrinkage caused by drying and aging.
**   The majority of early "Extra Lightweight" rifles were equipped with the hard rubber buttplate which had a pointed spur or tang to circa serial #145,000. After, they were made without the spur and the cut on the stock was eliminated.

The Models of 1886 and 1892

The pistol grip cap was oval in shape, 1 17/32 inches long at the longest point by 1 17/64 inches wide at its widest. The cap was rounded and rose 9/32 inches high, not including two protrusions on the bottom that fitted into corresponding recesses cut into the bottom of the grip. These protrusions were located on the bottom of the cap adjacent to the outer circumference of the screw hole and measured 5/16 inches long by 1/4 inches wide by 3/32 inches high. See Figure 4-13.

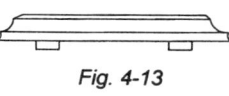

Fig. 4-13

The pistol grip cap had a screw hole 13/64 inches in diameter, countersunk to 11/32 inches in diameter in the center.

The pistol grip cap was secured by a small wood screw measuring from 63/64 inches to 1 1/64 inches long. It had a flat topped, bevel-shouldered head 5/16 inches in diameter and 3/32 inches high. Only the lower 19/32 inches of the shank of this screw was threaded. The head fitted into the countersunk screw hole in the cap to form a very close fit, flush with the outer surface. The screw head was usually, but not always, machine-engraved with a floral pattern, and was heat-blued. See Figure 4-14.

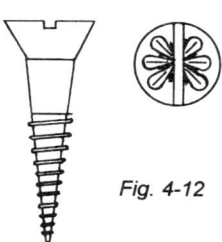

Fig. 4-12

NOTE: This same screw (with engraving) secured the hard rubber buttplate on the Winchester Model 1906 .22 caliber pump rifle, and on some late Model 1890 .22 pumps that were equipped with the 1906 style rubber buttplate. In fact, this screw and cap arrangement predominated on pistol grip variations of subsequent models that were fitted with the smaller size buttstocks similar in design, shape and dimensions as the Type 2 standard rifle stocks on late manufactured Model 1886 rifles.

Winchester Lever Action Repeaters

Carbine Buttstocks
Unlike rifle buttstocks, carbine buttstocks did not undergo a reduction in size during their production life. Measurements are shown in Table 4-6

But two types were produced and can be identified by the transition from wrist to comb: Type 1 carbine buttstocks were used on early carbines that were equipped with the Type 1 18 inch musket-style forearm. The transition from comb to wrist was nearly vertical to circa serial #30,000. See Figure 4-15.

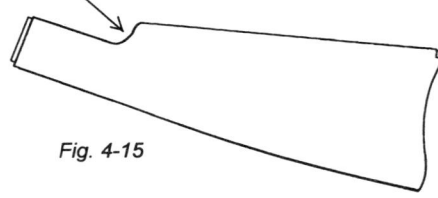
Fig. 4-15

Type 2 carbine buttstocks used after circa serial #30,000 showed a pronounced slope from comb to wrist. The collector can use this point to help determine if the stock on one of these very rare carbine variations is genuine. Most counterfeiters do not have access to the early M1886 carbine from which to make duplicates. See Figure 4-16.

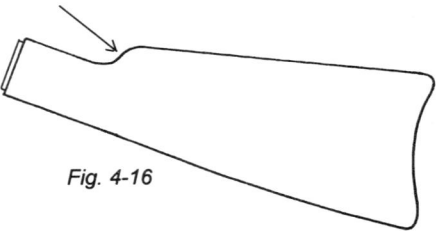
Fig. 4-16

NOTE: A mounting hole for the milling machine was also drilled into the end of carbine buttstocks. It was 1 7/8 inches deep by 45/64 inches in diameter.

Rear Sling Swivel
Sling swivels were a special order item. Winchester would install any type of sling swivel arrangement a customer wanted, but the most common was the "hook and eye". These were installed when the customer ordered sling swivels but did not specify the type.

The Models of 1886 and 1892

TABLE 4-6 CARBINE BUTTSTOCK MEASUREMENTS (ACCURACY ± 1/32 TO 1/4 INCHES)*	
AREA MEASURED	MEASUREMENT (INCHES)
Length across bottom (less lip at front)	13 7/8
Length across top (less lip at front)	13 5/16
Height, center of wrist	1 39/64
Width, center of wrist	1 716
Height at front of buttplate tang cutout	4 1/8
Height at extreme rear of buttstock	4 1/16
Width at extreme rear of buttstock	1 7/16
Width at center bulge	1 17/32

*Expected variation in actual measurements from those listed due to manufacturing tolerances and shrinking and drying of aged wood.

The sling hook eye was centered between the rounded sides of the stock and usually located about four inches forward of the buttplate. When properly installed at the Winchester factory, the flange will press against the wood without gaps.

The rear stud or "eye" for the Winchester sling which utilized the hook-style attaching mechanism was located in the underside of the buttstock on both rifles and carbines. The eye consisted of a wood screw, a bored-through eye offset to the top and a flange or base which was 19/64 inches in diameter by 1/32 inches high. See Figure 4-17.

Fig. 4-17

Winchester Lever Action Repeaters

The stud and eye were one inch long, overall. The shank was 11/16 inches long but threaded for only 17/32 inches of its length. The eye was 23/64 inches in diameter by 7/32 inches wide. It had an unthreaded hole, 3/16 inches diameter, bored through its center for attaching the sling hook.

NOTE: Originally installed eyes have been observed located forward of the buttplate anywhere from 2 1/16 inches to 4 13/16 inches. Variations of as much as 2 3/4 inches will be noted as there seems to have been no set specification for their placement.

Front sling swivels are described on page 80-81.

The Models of 1886 and 1892

Receivers

The M1886 receiver was milled from a single billet of steel. It was the first in the Winchester lever action line to have a solid bottom surface without the opening for the cartridge lifter. John Browning's design, a radical change for Winchester from the comparatively weak toggle link action employed previously, strengthened the receiver and allowed the use of more powerful cartridges. See Figure 4-18.

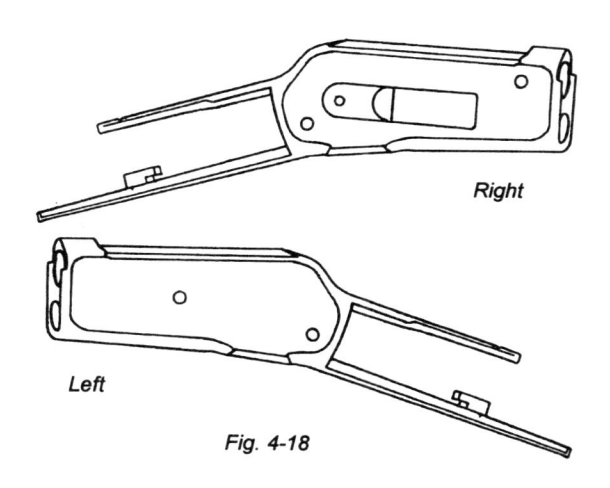

Right

Left

Fig. 4-18

The M1886 receiver was manufactured in three types which are described below and summarized in Table 4-7. **Type 1**: the height of the receiver at the front was 2 13/32 inches high from circa serial # 1-83,000.

Type 2: From circa serial #83,000 to the end of production, the height of the receiver at the front was reduced to 2 5/32 inches.

Type 3: the Model 1886 was the first Winchester Lever Action Repeater to incorporate the takedown variation as a readily-available

Winchester Lever Action Repeaters

option. It was introduced in late 1893 at circa serial #75,000 and was first listed in the Winchester catalog for 1894. While there had been a few Model 1873 factory-made takedown rifles—and all in 22 caliber—there were plenty of M1886 takedown rifles in a relatively wide variety of calibers. Even so, they command a considerable premium over a standard solid-frame model among today's collectors.

The M1886 receiver had three screw holes on the right side of the receiver. The rearmost was for the hammer screw. It was 17/64 inches in diameter and threaded 1/4-30. The middle hole was for the loading gate screw. The hole was 11/64 inches in diameter and threaded 3/16-36. The forward hole was for the cartridge guide screw. It was 19/64 inches in diameter, counterbored to 23/64 inches and unthreaded.

The M1886 receiver had two holes on the left side of the receiver. The rearmost was for the hammer screw. It was 17/64 inches in diameter, counterbored to a depth of 3/32 inches, and 19/64 inches in diameter and unthreaded. The hammer screw entered from the left side of the receiver, passed through the hammer and threaded into the right side of the receiver with only the tip visible.

The forward screw hole was for the cartridge stop screw. It was 9/32 inches in diameter, counterbored to 3/16 inches and was unthreaded.

M1886 receivers can also be distinguished by the number of screw holes in the upper tang. Early receivers to circa serial #19,500-23,500 have three screw holes. The first for the tang sight, the second for the carrier spring screw and the third for the stock bolt. After circa serial #19,500-23,500, the second screw hole was not drilled all the way through and a shorter carrier spring screw was used. Refer to Upper Tang on page 30.

The Type 3 takedown receiver was quite different from the non-takedown receiver in that the front, or face, of the receiver was flat

The Models of 1886 and 1892

where it mates with the takedown extension. The takedown receiver was also considerably shorter than the non-takedown receiver when the extension was ignored but if measured with the extension in place, then the receiver will be slightly longer. Therefore, a non-takedown gun cannot be made into a takedown.

The takedown variation was made in two sub-variations: **Type 3A** was 2 13/64 ± 1/32 inches high at the barrel junction to circa serial #83,000; after, the **Type 3B** was 2 5/32 ± 1/32 inches high at the barrel junction to the end of production.

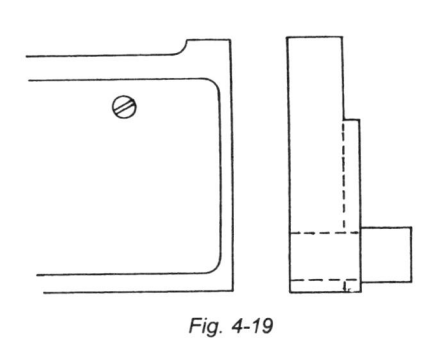

Takedown Receiver Extension

The dimensions for the takedown extension were 1/2 ± 1/64 inches long (not including the magazine tube guide), 1 13/32 ± 1/64 inches wide, 2 5/32 ± 1/32 inches high. The length at the top, less the cut-out for the barrel, was 25/64 inches with no apparent deviation. See Figure 4-19.

Fig. 4-19

The magazine tube guide extended into the forearm 23/32 inches and protruded beyond the front of the extension 3/8 inches. It had an outside diameter of 27/32 inches and an inside diameter of 11/16 inches. 7/16 inches of its circumference was cut out at the top (arrow), just under the barrel. See Figure 4-20.

The takedown extension adjusted to the receiver face with three screws, Figure 4-21. These

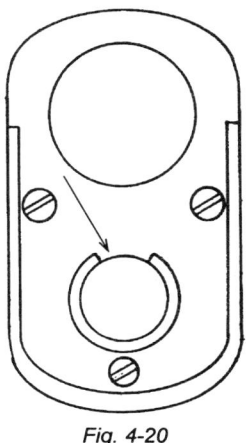

Fig. 4-21

Fig. 4-20

Winchester Lever Action Repeaters

TABLE 4-7 RECEIVER DIMENSIONS (INCHES)	
Standard Receiver Pre-1894 (1 to circa s/# 83,000)	
Length of receiver face to junction with upper tang	6 3/8
Front edge of loading port to front of receiver	1 49/64
Width (immediately behind forend	1 13/64 ± 1/64 *
Width (at stock wrist socket)	1 13/32 ± 1/64
Height (at barrel junction)	2 13/64 ± 1/32
Height (at stock wrist socket)	2 13/32 ± 1/32
Loading gate cutout	1 inch forward of the receiver stock socket. The cutout was 3 17/64 ± 1/32 inches long by 11/16 ± 1/64 inches high
Takedown Receiver Pre-1894 (1 to circa s/#83,000) minus extension	
Length of receiver face to junction with upper tang	6 1/8
Front edge of loading port to front of receiver	1 43/64
Width (immediately behind forend	1 13/64 ± 1/64
Width (at stock wrist socket)	1 13/32 ± 1/64
Height (at barrel junction)	2 13/64 ± 1/32
Height (at stock wrist socket)	2 13/32 ± 1/32

The Models of 1886 and 1892

Loading gate cutout	1 inch forward of the receiver stock socket. The cutout was 3 17/64 ± 1/32 inches long by 11/16 ± 1/64 inches high
Standard Receiver Post-1894 (c s/# 83,000 to end of production) **	
Height (at barrel junction)	2 5/32 ± 1/32
Takedown Receiver Post-1894 (circa s/# 83,000 to end of production) minus extension **	
Height (at barrel junction)	2 5/32 ± 1/32
* The tolerance variations in these dimensions are the result of the polish applied to the receiver before finishing. ** Other receiver dimensions remain the same as pre-1894 receivers	

headless screws were 23/64 inches long overall, 3/16 inches in diameter and had a 9/64 inch diameter unthreaded projection on the end 5/64 inches long.

A partial thread on the barrel socket matched the interrupted threads on the takedown barrel. The barrel socket threads were machined in the form of arcs at the top and bottom. They were cut 20 threads to the inch. Refer to Takedown barrels on page 72.

Receiver—Finish

The standard receiver finish for the non-takedown M1886 rifle and carbine was color case hardening to circa serial #122,000. Color case hardening for takedown frames was the standard finish until circa serial #90,000. After these serial number ranges, the standard finish was bluing, but color case hardened receivers could still be had on special order.

M1886 color case hardened receivers lost their bright colors easily compared to the color case-hardened M1873 and M1876 receivers.

Winchester Lever Action Repeaters

Winchester used a new steel with nickel and chromium added as alloying agents. The high heat required for the case hardening process caused the chromium and nickel molecules to migrate to just below the surface. As the case colors faded, the receiver turned a silvery color that appeared similar to nickel plating.

NOTE: Color case hardened receivers always command a considerable premium over blued receivers, primarily as it denotes an older and therefore, more desirable firearm to the collector.

Upper Tang

The M1886 upper tang was an integral part of the receiver It was 3 29/32 inches long, 29/32 inches wide at its widest point at the junction with the receiver and tapered to 1/2 inch wide at the extreme rear. The upper tang had three screw holes. See Figure 4-22.

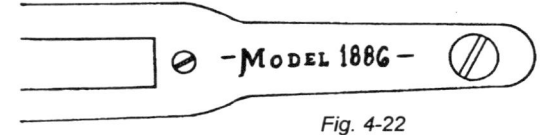

Fig. 4-22

Upper Tang Screws and Screw Holes
The first screw hole was for the add-on tang sight. It was 9/16 inches behind the hammer slot, was threaded 3/16-36 and was plugged with a headless plug screw 7/32 inches long by 3/16 inches in diameter when a tang sight was not mounted. This screw hole was very rarely omitted on the M1886—except on special order— and when it was, may have been an oversight.

The second screw hole was for the "carrier spring screw" which secured the carrier spring to the underside of the upper tang. It was 7/32 inches behind the tang sight plug screw. Until circa serial #19,500-23,500, the carrier spring screw hole was bored through the upper tang. After, it ended in a blind hole and was not visible. The carrier spring and carrier spring screws are described on page 52.

The Models of 1886 and 1892

The *head* of the carrier spring screw was never visible—only the shank end could be seen and then only prior to circa serial #19,500-23,500 as it was inserted from beneath the tang.

NOTE: The National Rifle Association's excellent publication, "Firearms Assembly: The N.R.A. Guide to Rifles and Shotguns," Model 1886 exploded view has misidentified the carrier spring (No. 25) as the carrier stop. The screw that holds it in place (No. 26) was incorrectly identified as the carrier stop screw, but is in fact, the carrier spring screw.

The stock bolt, also known as the tang screw, passed through the third screw hole which was located 7/16 inches from the rear of the upper tang and was unthreaded. The screw hole was 15/64 inches in diameter and countersunk to 23/64 inches in diameter.

NOTE: Any hole drilled and tapped in the upper tang that interfered with the Winchester markings was non-factory in origin. Non-factory modifications reduce the collector's value considerably.

Model Markings
Model markings were roll stamped on the upper tang on all variations of the M1886 with the exception of the very last guns after circa serial #159,000, made up out of parts on hand after production had ceased.

The first style of upper tang marking used from the start of production until circa serial #120,000 read

—Model 1886—

The line was 1 1/2 inches long in block letters with serifs. The first stroke of the "M" was 13/64 inches long and fell below the bottom line but did not overlap the dash that preceded it. The rest of the "M" and the numbers in the model marking were 11/64 inches high and the letters "ODEL" were 5/64 inches high.

Winchester Lever Action Repeaters

The second style markings appeared at circa serial #120,000 and read

MODEL 1886
—WINCHESTER—
TRADE MARK

The top line was in block letters with serifs and numbers 3/32 inches high. The line was 1 17/32 inches long. The second line was also in block letters with serifs 5/32 inches high, and was 1 25/32 inches long including the dashes. The serifs on the first and last letters overlapped the dashes slightly. The bottom line was in smaller block letters without serifs 1/16 inches high. The line was 13/16 inches long.

The third style of marking appeared at circa serial #150,000. Reflecting the company's problems with patent infringements, it read

MODEL 1886
—WINCHESTER—
TRADE MARK REG. IN U.S. PAT. OFF.

The top line was in block letters and numbers with serifs 3/32 inches high. The line was 1 17/32 inches long. The second line was also in block letters with serifs 5/32 inches high, and was 1 21/32 inches long including the dashes. The serifs on the first and last letters overlapped the dashes slightly. The bottom line was in smaller block letters without serifs 1/16 inches high and was 1 37/64 inches long. As the 19th Century came to a close, the first two digits in the model year, "18", were sometimes dropped. The line length remained the same but a gap was left because of the missing digits.

The fourth style of marking was used with the last Model 1886s after circa serial #159,000 which were made up from parts after production ended. The marking was similar to that found on the continuation Model 71.

WINCHESTER
TRADE MARK
MADE IN U.S.A.

The Models of 1886 and 1892

Markings on these very late guns were so varied—and so rarely encountered—on the Model 1886 that it is impossible to state exactly how they were marked. The only constant was the Winchester name, and even its position varied between the top and center lines. The lower line may have been omitted altogether and/or its position may have been shifted upward.

Lower Tang

The lower tang was a separate assembly held to the receiver by the hammer screw (also referred to as the receiver screw). Metallurgical analysis conducted by John Madl, CmfgE, of Lake Superior State University at Sault Ste, Marie, Michigan indicates that the lower tang, like the receiver, was forged of mild steel to approximate shape, then machined to final size.

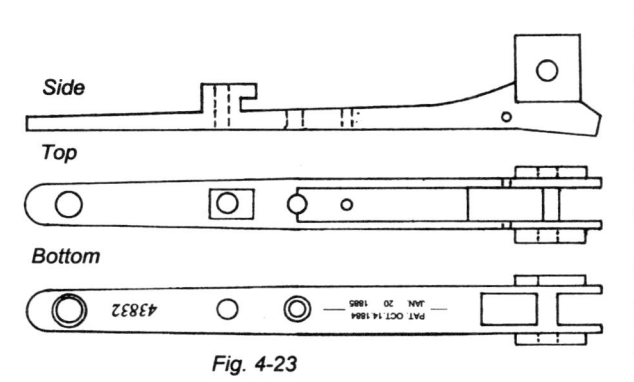

Fig. 4-23

The standard lower tang was the straight, non-pistol grip tang. It was 6 5/8 inches long and had four holes, one slot and one cutout. See Figure 4-23.

The rearmost hole for the lower tang screw was 15/64 inches in diameter, was unthreaded, countersunk and located 1/2 inches forward of the tang's rear. The lower tang screw (wood) was 27/32 inches long with an oval head and was slightly shorter than the buttplate screw.

The stock bolt hole was 1 11/16 inches forward of the lower tang screw hole. It was 13/64 inches in diameter, had a 12-28 thread. The upper

Winchester Lever Action Repeaters

tang screw passed through the upper tang, the stock wrist and threaded into the mainspring mounting stud on the inside of the lower tang.

The M1886 stock bolt was 1 25/32 inches long overall, had an oval head 1/8 inches high and 11/32 inches in diameter. The shank was 13/64 inches in diameter and threaded for 23/64 inches of its length with a 12-28 thread. When installed at the factory, an original M1886 stock bolt tip was flush with the outer surface of the lower tang. Stock bolts for the Models of 1873, 1876, 1892, 1894, and 1895 will fit but were shorter and will appear to be recessed in the lower tang. See Figure 4-24.

Fig. 4-24 The mainspring strain screw hole was 7/8 inches forward of the stock bolt hole. It was 11/64 inches in diameter, counterbored and threaded 9-32. The mainspring strain screw (also called the mainspring tension screw) had a fillister head. It was 19/64 inches long and its head was 1/16 inches high and 3/16 inches in diameter. The screw shank was only 11/64 inches in diameter, quite large in relation to the diameter of the head. The screw had two purposes: it pressed against the bottom of the mainspring to adjust the force of the hammer fall and it kept the mainspring in place in the groove cut into the mainspring stud.

The mainspring stud was located 1 49/64 inches from the rear of the lower tang. It was 13/32 inches wide by 19/64 inches high. A cut was made in the forward surface to hold the end of the mainspring. The cut was 9/64 inches deep and 3/16 inches long. The mainspring stud was drilled through its center for the stock bolt and the hole was threaded 12-28.

The trigger and sear spring screw hole was 37/64 inches forward of the mainspring strain screw hole. It was 9/64 inches in diameter and had a 6-48 thread. The trigger and sear spring screw threaded into the tang from the inside and was 1/4 inches long. The screw had a fillister

The Models of 1886 and 1892

head with unbeveled shoulders, 3/16 inches in diameter and 5/64 inches high. The shank of the screw was 11/64 inches long, 9/64 inches in diameter and had a 6-48 thread. It held the sear and trigger spring in a milled groove on the inside surface of the lower tang. The shank end of a factory-original and properly installed screw was always flush with the surface of the lower tang, just behind the patent dates.

The trigger slot was 1 11/16 inches forward of the center of the trigger spring screw hole, was rectangular in shape, was 41/64 inches long by 25/64 inches wide, and was cut through the tang.

The finger lever cutout was 17/64 inches forward of the trigger slot. It was 3/8 inches long by 29/64 inches wide and formed the rear of the finger lever opening in the bottom of the receiver.

There were two holes in the sides of the lower tang. The first, for the trigger pin, was unthreaded and penetrated both side flanges of the tang. It was 1/8 inches in diameter and located exactly one inch from the front of the tang.

The second hole was for the hammer screw. It was 17/32 inches from the front, was 17/64 inches in diameter, unthreaded and the screw hole penetrated both sides of the receiver and both vertical flanges on the lower tang in the receiver.

The hammer screw was 1 15/64 inches long overall, had a fillister head 7/64 inches high by 9/32 inches in diameter. The hammer screw shank was 1/4 inches in diameter and had a 1/4-30 thread on the lower 11/32 inches. The hammer screw threaded into the right side of the receiver.

In all, a total of thirteen variations of the M1886 lower tang have been identified to date. Table 4-8 lists each with its identifying characteristics and estimated serial number range. As usual, expect a wide variance in serial number range.

Winchester Lever Action Repeaters

TABLE 4-8
M1886 LOWER TANG VARIATIONS

No.	Grip Type	Tang Type	Trigger Type	Inlay/Cap	Wood Screw	Circa Serial #
1	Straight	Square	Plain	None	Yes	0-3000 to 4,000
2	Straight	Reinforced	Plain	None	Yes	3,000 to 4,000 to EOP
3	Straight	Square	SST	None	Yes	0-3,000 to 5,000
4	Straight	Reinforced	SST	None	Yes	3,000 to 5,000 to 100,000
5	Straight	Reinforced	DST	None	Yes	100,000 to EOP
6	Pistol	Square	Plain	Inlay	Yes	0-3,000-4,000
7	Pistol	Reinforced	Plain	Inlay	Yes	3,000-4,000 to 100,000
8	Pistol	Reinforced	Plain	Cap	No	100,000 to EOP
9	Pistol	Square	SST	Inlay	Yes	0-3,000-4000
10	Pistol	Reinforced	SST	Inlay	Yes	3,000-4,000 to 100,000
11	Pistol	Reinforced	SST	Cap	No	100,000 to 120,000
12	Pistol	Reinforced	DST	Inlay	Yes	100,000 to 120,000
13	Pistol	Reinforced	DST	Cap	No	100,000 to EOP

SST: Single Set Trigger   DST: Double Set Trigger   EOP: End of Production
Information in this table was provided through courtesy of John Madl, CmfgE, Lake Superior State University, Sault Ste. Marie, Michigan

The Models of 1886 and 1892

Patent Markings
The patent dates were marked on the lower tang directly behind the trigger slot from the beginning of production until circa serial #143,000. They read from front to rear in block letters without serifs

___ PAT. OCT.14.1884 ___
Jan.   20.   1885

The unusual spacing was probably an attempt by Winchester to produce lines of equal length. The top and bottom lines were 51/64 inches long (not including dashes which were centered vertically between the lines) and the letters and numbers 5/64 inches high. After circa serial #143,000, the patent dates on the lower tang were considered redundant as the same dates were included in the barrel address markings starting at circa serial #140,000. At this point, the patent dates were deleted from the lower tang to the end of production.

Serial Numbers
Serial numbers were stamped on the lower tang on all variations of the Model 1886. They were centered between the lower tang screw *hole* and the upper tang screw *hole* throughout production. They were marked in three styles of type.

To circa serial #120,000, the serial numbers were lightly stamped to read from front to rear in italic numbers with serifs 5/32 inches high.

5432

From circa serial #120,000 to circa serial #145,000, the serial numbers were stamped with more pressure. The numbers were italic style with serifs and smaller at 9/64 inches high.

123456

The third and last style serial number stampings were used from circa serial #145,000 to the end of production. They were stamped in block letters with serifs 1/8 inches high.

145678

For a list of serial numbers by year, see Appendix A.

Winchester Lever Action Repeaters

Assembly Numbers
Assembly numbers are rarely found on the standard production M1886 and when they are, no particular pattern can be discerned. Most special order M1886s with buttstocks other than standard, will show assembly numbers. The assembly number was always located on the left side of the lower tang. The same number was repeated on the stock wrist in the upper tang cutout, and most often, but not always, on the toe of the buttplate.

An assembly number appearing on the rare M1886 with a standard buttstock, may or may not have the assembly number on the stock and almost never on the buttplate toe. This was particularly true of special order M1886s with set triggers but no other special order features.

Safety Catch
There was no safety catch or trigger bar on the Model 1886 as it employed a safety device linked to the travel of the locking bolts that blocked the hammer from striking the firing pin. This safety functioned automatically and was very effective. The M1886 could not be fired unless the finger lever was closed and the locking bolts were in their proper position.

Pistol Grip Lower Tang
The pistol grip lower tang was slightly shorter than the straight grip lower tang. It was 4 3/4 inches ± 1/16 inches long when measured forward edge to the rear of the tang or 4 7/8 inches ± 1/16 inches measured along the curve. See Figure 4-25.

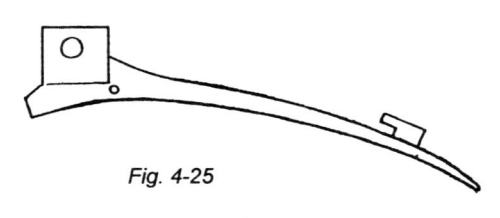

Fig. 4-25

Pistol grip tangs were straight tangs bent to shape in a fixture, according to Winchester drawing number 2197, dated October 27, 1886. This information was recently uncovered in the Cody Firearms

The Models of 1886 and 1892

Museum archives by John Madl, CmfgE, of Lake Superior State Univeristy at Sault Ste, Marie, Michigan.

A variation of the pistol grip lower tang lacked the hole at the extreme rear for the lower tang screw. The lower tang was only 4 1/2 inches ± 1/16 inches long but remained the same as the standard pistol grip lower tang in all other dimensions. Winchester shortened the pistol grip lower tang so the grip of the stock would not be too long.

The mainspring stud was located in the same place on the lower tang of both pistol grip variations as on the straight grip lower tang. This made it possible to use the same mainspring for all three types simply by shaping the mainspring to the different profile before heat treating and tempering.

NOTE: The separate lower tang on the M1886 makes it possible for an unscrupulous person to switch serial numbered lower tangs from one gun to another, or to install a pistol grip or other special order feature. Exercise caution when examining any M1886 rifle or carbine. The lower tang should exhibit a similar degree of wear and remaining finish as the rest of the receiver. If an assembly number was stamped on the pistol grip tang, make certain that it also appears on the buttstock. It was sometimes also stamped on the buttplate toe.

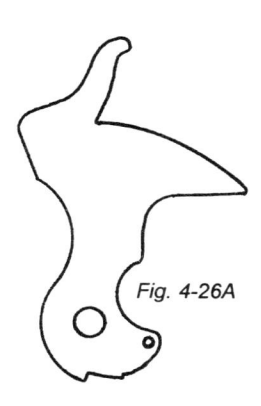

Fig. 4-26A

Hammers

The M1886 hammer was 3/8 inches wide, 2 23/32 inches tall and 1 3/4 inches front to back at its longest point. The Model 1886 hammer used the same stirrup or hammer link and retaining pin as the other lever action repeating models with the notable exception of the Model 1895 which used a roller mounted in the base of the hammer. See Figure 4-26A.

Winchester Lever Action Repeaters

Color case-hardened hammers predominate throughout M1886 production. Other finishes were applied to hammers only on special order. After circa serial number #150,000, blued hammers were occasionally used but usually in conjunction with blued receivers.

There were three basic styles of M1886 hammer knurling. See Figure 4-26B. The **Type 1** hammer used to circa serial number 35,000 had a fine knurl with a relatively large diamond pattern. The Type 1 hammers were eight diamonds wide. The knurled area was 21/64 inches wide by 23/64 inches long at the right and left edges.

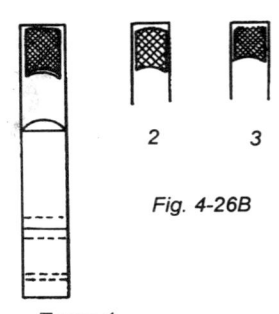

Type 2 hammers appeared at circa serial number 35,000. Winchester shifted to a coarser pattern, but similar to the first type. Both the first and second type knurling were used sporadically until circa serial number 140,000. The Type 2 hammers were seven diamonds wide. The knurled area was 21/64 inches wide by 11/32 inches long at the right and left edges.

Fig. 4-26B

Types 1 2 3

At circa serial #140,000, the **Type 3** hammer was introduced. The border surrounding the knurling was similar to the first type, but smaller. The second and third style were in use at the same time until the end of production, although the second style dwindled in frequency as the production came to an end. The Type 3 hammers were 7 diamonds wide. The knurled area was 11/32 inches wide by 25/64 inches long at the right and left edges.

Hammer Screw
The hammer was held in the frame by a "receiver screw" (modern collectors refer to it as a hammer screw. The hammer screw was 1 15/64 inches long overall with a shank 1 1/8 inches long and 1/4 inch in diameter. Its fillister head was 7/64 inches high and 9/32 inches in diameter. The end of the shank was threaded (1/4-30) for 11/32 inches of its length, the same thread size as used on all saddle ring studs on all

The Models of 1886 and 1892

models using the threaded single-shank style saddle ring stud (M1876, M1886, M1894 and M1895).

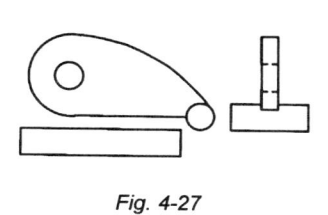

Stirrup and Pin

The stirrup connected the hammer to the main spring. It was a thin, rounded piece of steel 35/64 inches long by 5/64 inches thick with a round crosspiece at the tail which engaged the main spring's "claws". The crosspiece was 19/64 inches long by 7/64 inches in diameter. See Figure 4-27.

Fig. 4-27

Trigger/Sear

The Model 1886 incorporated a one-piece trigger and sear mechanism which was identical to and interchangeable with the Model 1892 trigger and sear. The trigger/sear was 1 3/4 inches long when the curve of the trigger finger piece is taken into consideration. The sear part of the trigger mechanism was 1.0 inches long and 3/8 inches wide while the trigger itself was 31/32 inches long by 9/32 inches wide at the top with a very slight taper to 17/64 inches wide at the tip. Figure 4-28.

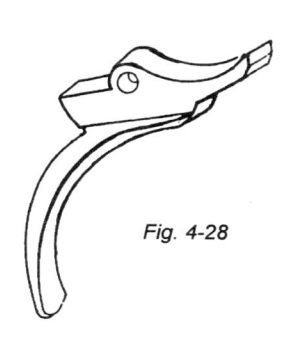

Fig. 4-28

The trigger/sear had a 9/64 inches diameter hole drilled tangentially through the body of the sear to facilitate installing the mechanism in the action with the trigger pin.

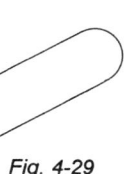

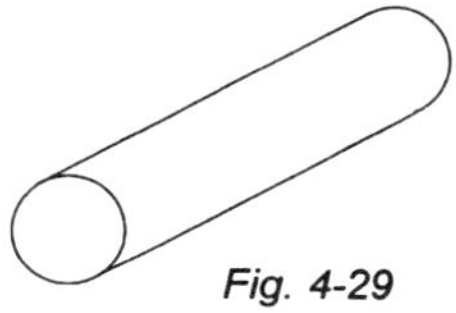

Fig. 4-29

The trigger/sear was held in the receiver by the trigger pin which was a straight pin made of case hardened steel 43/64 inches long by 1/8 inches in diameter. The pin was press-fitted into the sides of the lower tang. See Figure 4-29.

Winchester Lever Action Repeaters

Trigger Spring and Screw
The trigger spring was flat spring steel, 3/64 inches thick. It was 1 51/64 inches long by 3/8 inches wide at the mounting end, tapering to 9/32 inches wide at the action end where it bore on the camming flat at the base of the sear. The spring had a 9/64 inches diameter unthreaded hole at the wide end for installation using the trigger spring screw. The trigger spring screw was 1/4 inches long by 1/8 inches in diameter and was threaded 6-48. The head was 13/64 inches in diameter and 1/16 inches high. See Figure 4-30.

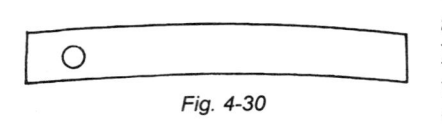

Fig. 4-30

Finger Lever
The M1886 finger lever was 8 5/16 inches long by 29/64 inches wide by 1 19/64 ± 1/32 inches high. The inside finger loop was 2 41/64 inches long by 63/64 ± 1/32 inches high. The inside trigger loop was 1 17/32 inches long by 59/64 inches high.

All finger levers were color case hardened to circa serial #152,000. After, blued finger levers were occasionally installed on standard guns. Blued levers were available on special order throughout production, but were rarely ordered.

The M1886 finger lever had five holes. From muzzle to rear they were: 1) Lever and breechblock pin hole, 3/16 inches in diameter, 2) Carrier hook stud hole, 3/16 inches in diameter, 3) Finger lever bushing hole which was oblong in shape and 5/16 inches wide by 31/32 inches long, 4) Friction stud or lever catch hole, 17/64 inches in diameter and 7/8 inches deep, 5) Friction stud pin hole to retain the friction stud, 5/64 inches in diameter.

The M1886 finger lever lacked the projections found on the late M1866, the M1873 and the M1876 finger levers which activated the trigger bar safety mechanism. It also lacked the "anvil-like" rear projection to the finger lever catch as the M1886 used the friction stud rather than the swiveling finger lever catch.

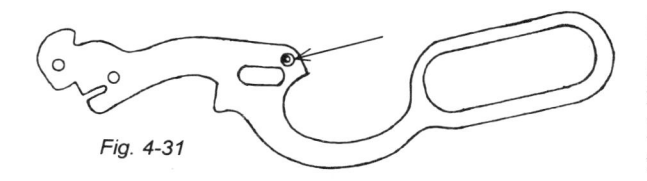

The Models of 1886 and 1892

Fig. 4-31

Four types of finger levers were made for the M1886. **Type 1** finger levers have the friction stud and spring which served as the lever catch installed on the left rear side of the trigger loop to circa serial number 14,000. The hole for the friction stud was 17/64 inches in diameter and 11/32 ± 1/32 inches deep. See Figure 4-31.

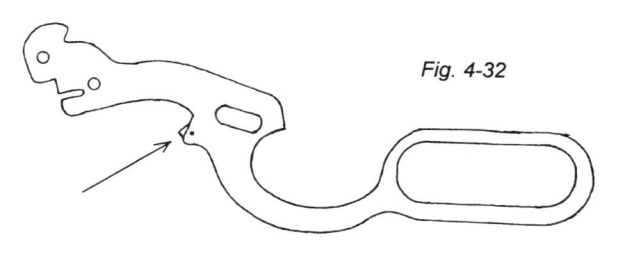

Type 2 finger levers made after circa serial #14,000 were identical to the Type 1 except that the lever catch (friction stud and spring) was installed in front of the trigger loop. The hole for the friction stud catch was 17/64 inches in diameter and 7/8 inches deep. See Figure 4-32.

Fig. 4-32

Type 1 and Type 2 finger levers were interchangeable, although they may not lock up as tightly if interchanged due to the different friction stud locations.

Type 3 finger levers were made for those rifles fitted with a pistol grip stock. The type 3 finger lever was identical in all respects to the Type 1 or Type 2 finger lever except that it was bent, or formed, to the contour of the pistol grip. See Figure 4-33.

Type 4 finger levers installed on .50 caliber rifles and carbines had a milled-out section on the right side just in front of the carrier hook to allow the loading gate to swing inward far enough to accommodate the larger diameter .50 caliber cartridge. See Appendix D.

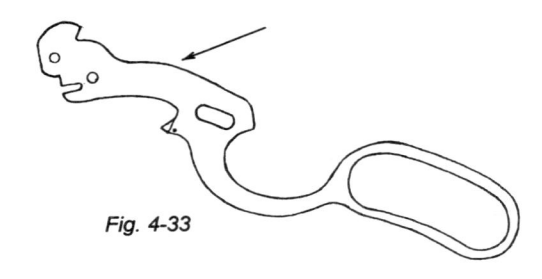

Winchester Lever Action Repeaters

Fig. 4-33

Friction Stud Lever Catch
The 3/16 inch long friction stud consisted of a spring-loaded plunger set into the left front side of the Type 1 finger lever trigger loop to circa serial #14,000. After, it was set into the top, front side and was 13/32 inches long. See Figure 4-34.

The hole for the friction stud was 17/64 inches in diameter. The hole in the Type 1 finger lever was 11/32 inches deep, that in the Type 2 was 7/8 inches deep. The plunger was 1/4 inch in diameter by 19/32 inches long. It had a notch in its upper surface 11/64 inches wide for the friction stud pin.

Fig. 4-34

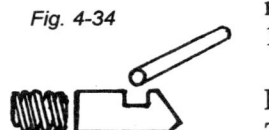

Friction Stud Spring and Pin
The friction stud spring was made from steel wire 1/64 inches in diameter. It was wound into a coil spring 13/64 inches in diameter and had 5 coils. The friction stud pin was 27/64 inches long and 5/64 inches in diameter, 1/32 inches shorter than the lever width which left the pin recessed 1/64 inch on each side. It was the same diameter as the hole and was press-fitted into place.

Saddle Ring and Stud
The M1886 saddle ring (Figure 4-35A) was identical to those used on all other Winchester Lever Action Repeaters. The outer diameter was 1 1/16 inches and the inner diameter was 23/32 inches. The ring was made of iron wire, 11/64 inches in diameter. The ends of the ring were pressed together, but not soldered or welded. Over the years, rust or corrosion may cause them to appear as if they were.

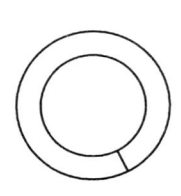

Fig. 35A

The saddle ring stud was similar to that used on the M1876, M1894 and M1895 Lever Action repeaters, Figure 4-35B. It was the screw-in type saddle ring stud

The Models of 1886 and 1892

that originated with the M1876. The saddle ring stud was located 1 1/8 inches forward of the upper tang/receiver juncture or 23/32 inches (center to center) ahead and above the hammer screw hole at an angle of 335 degrees.

The saddle ring stud was 29/64 inches long from the top of the loop to the base, was 31/64 inches in diameter at the base and threaded 1/4-30 thread for 13/64 inches from the end.

The saddle ring stud was interchangeable with those used on the M1894 and M1895 (threaded for only 3/32 inches from the end) but not the M1876.

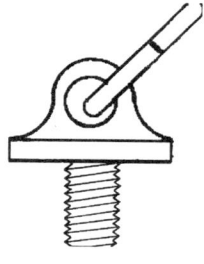

Fig. 4-35B

NOTE: While the saddle ring stud is nearly identical with that used on the M1876, the M1876 stud is too long and will press against the left hand locking bolt on the M1886, jamming the action. It is relatively easy to tell if a M1876 saddle ring stud has been shortened to fit. It will either be loose because of the unthreaded 1/4 inch portion of the shank immediately below the flange, or the threads will have been recut to make it fit properly. If you have any doubts, remove the stud and examine it carefully for evidence of shortening and rethreading. Also, beware of reproduction saddle ring studs which are plentiful. Counterfeit rings can be detected by careful measurement and observation. New-made rings will be relatively unmarred and retain most of their blued finish. Fortunately, replaced saddle rings do not appreciably affect collector value.

Breechbolts

The M1886 breechbolt was exactly 5 inches long, 3/4 inches high and 27/32 inches wide. The ejector housing protruded 5/32 inches beyond the forward end. See Figure 4-36A.

The cutout on the top surface of the breechbolt for the extractor was centered from side to side and was 2 13/16 inches long, 5/32 inches

Winchester Lever Action Repeaters

wide and 1/8 inches deep. The extractor cut deepened to 9/32 inches two-thirds of the distance to the rear to accommodate the extractor pin hole stud, then tapered upward to the top surface at the rear.

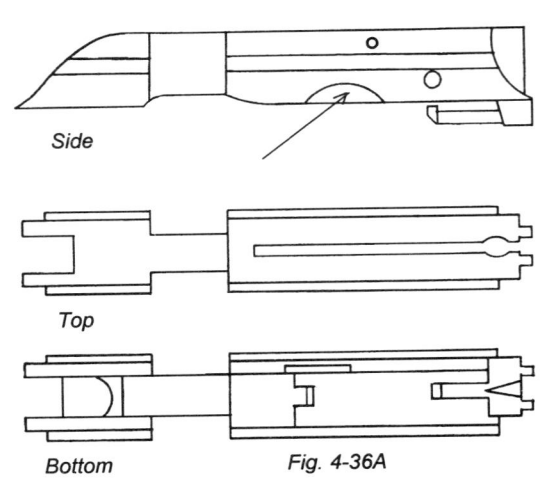

Side

Top

Bottom

Fig. 4-36A

The firing pin tunnel was drilled the length of the breech bolt. It was 7/64 inches in diameter at the forward face and 21/64 inches in diameter at the rear face.

Channels were milled on either side of the breechbolt, 3/4 inches long by 15/64 inches deep—including the side rails—to receive the left and right hand locking bolts.

Breechbolts had 3/32 inch square side rails machined into their right and left sides nearly the full length of the bolt. The rails fitted into corresponding grooves milled into the inside walls of the receiver. Lubricate these grooves and rails often as they are a friction fit.

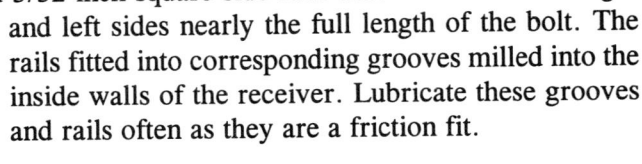

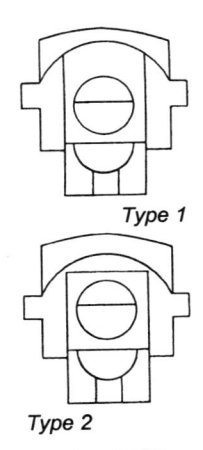

Type 1

Type 2

Fig. 4-36B

From the start of production to circa serial #11,000, the rear, vertical face of the breechbolt had a square appearance; after, it was rounded. See Figure 4-36B.

Two types of breechbolts were installed in the Model 1886. **Type 1** breechbolts were used almost exclusively from the start of production to circa serial #110,000, and intermittently thereafter to the end of production. Type 1 breechbolts had two holes bored

46

The Models of 1886 and 1892

across the width. The forward hole, 1 inch behind the breechbolt face, was 3/16 inches in diameter and was for the finger lever/breechbolt pin. The second hole was 1 7/8 inches behind the breechbolt face, was 3/32 inches in diameter and was for the extractor pin.

Type 2 breechbolts were used after circa serial #110,000 to the end of production and were identical to the Type 1 breechbolt except for a third hole drilled across the width for the firing pin stop pin. It was 3/32 inches in diameter, 1 3/32 inches ahead of the breech bolt *rear* face.

Model 1886 breechbolts were always blued, even during the color case hardening years. They often appear in better shape than the rest of the gun because of their recessed location atop the receiver.

NOTE: Some of the last M1886s were assembled using the M71 bolt and cartridge guide. The M71 cartridge guide lacks the top spur and the M71 bolt lacks the cutout for the cartridge guide spur on the right side (refer to arrows in Figures 4-36A and 4-49A). While the M1886 and M71 bolt and cartridge guide are interchangeable, the gun will only function when the two parts are installed as a set, i.e, M1886 bolt and cartridge guide or M71 bolt and cartridge guide, together.

Finger Lever/Breechbolt Pin
The finger lever/breechbolt pin was case-hardened steel, 21/32 inches long by 11/64 inches in diameter. The pin was 1/64 inches smaller in diameter than its hole so that it could rotate freely and act as a pivot point for the finger lever. This pin was ground and polished flat on each end and fitted flush with the outer surfaces of the breechbolt when properly installed. See Figure 4-37.

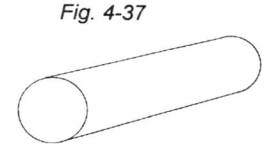

Fig. 4-37

Bent, corroded, or damaged finger lever/breechbolt pins make the action difficult to operate. Improperly fitted replacement or reproduction pins can wear against the inner surface

Winchester Lever Action Repeaters

of the receiver producing a "sticky action." As this pin is difficult to install properly, many were often hammered into place during non-factory repairs.

Extractor Pin
The extractor was secured into the cutout in the upper surface of the breechbolt by a single pin press-fitted into a hole drilled crosswise 1 7/8 inches behind the bolt face. The extractor pin was made of case-hardened steel wire and was 21/32 inches long by 3/32 inches in diameter. The ends of the extractor pin were flush with the breechbolt side surfaces when properly installed. See Figure 4-38.

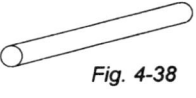

Fig. 4-38

Firing Pin Stop Pin
The firing pin stop pin was installed only on the Type 2 M1886 breechbolt (circa serial #110,000). It was 21/32 inches long by 3/32 inches in diameter, was press-fitted and was ground and polished so that it was flush with the sides of the breechbolt when properly installed. See Figure 4-39.

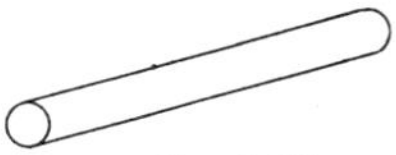

Fig. 4-39

Locking Bolts
The M1886 breechbolt was locked in the firing position by two breechbolt locking bolts (one on either side of the bolt). When the action was closed, the locking bolts were rotated up through grooves on the inside of the receiver and into cutouts on either side of the bolt. See Figure 4-40.

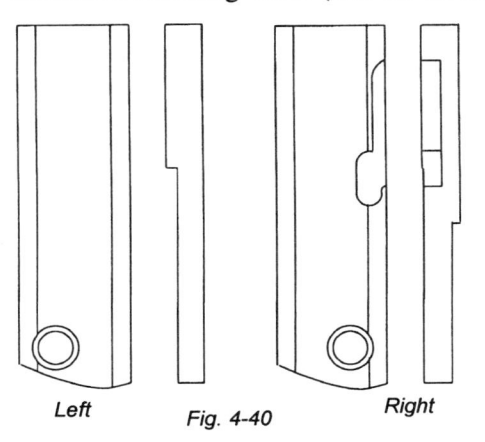

The locking bolts were 3/4 inches wide by 2 29/64 inches high by 1/4 inches thick. The top end that locked the

Left   Fig. 4-40   Right

The Models of 1886 and 1892

breechbolt in the firing position was 1/4 inches thick. The opposite end was milled to 7/32 inches wide for only 1 29/64 inches of its length.

The locking bolts were made of high-carbon steel, milled from single blocks and hardened for strength.

The locking bolts were raised into the upper, or locked, position by the finger lever bearing on the finger lever bushing and the finger lever bushing pin. The *pin and bushing assembly* were installed through 21/64 inch diameter, unthreaded, counterbored holes in the lower part of the locking bolts and through an elliptically cut hole in the finger lever itself. The *finger lever bushing* provided both the pivoting surface for the locking bolt and attached the finger lever to the locking bolts. It was 5/16 inches in diameter and 51/64 inches long. It had a flange 11/32 inches in diameter by 3/64 inches long on one end to secure it to the locking bolts. See Figure 4-41.

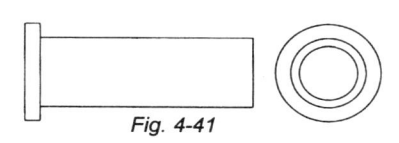

Fig. 4-41

A separate *finger lever bushing pin*—sometimes called the split pin—secured the finger lever bushing in place. It was 55/64 inches long by 13/64 inches in diameter and had flanges on either end. The head end flange was 1/4 inch in diameter by 3/64 inches long. The flange on the split end was 11/64 inches in diameter by 3/64 inches long. It was split 1/16 inch wide for 5/8 inches of its length to facilitate installation through the center of the hollow finger lever bushing. See Figure 4-42.

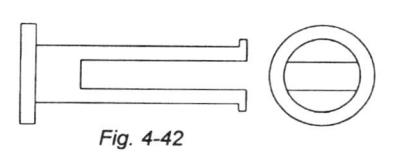

Fig. 4-42

The flange on the bushing kept it from backing out one way and the flange on the bushing pin kept it from backing out the other way. Both flanges fit snugly into counterbores in pivot holes in the locking bolts.

Winchester Lever Action Repeaters

To remove the finger lever bushing, the ends of the *bushing pin* must be pinched together, then pushed out. The finger lever bushing was then pushed out of the locking bolt holes in the direction of the flange.

Extractor

The Model 1886 extractor was mounted in a groove centered in the top surface of the breechbolt. The extractor was 3 inches long, 9/64 inches wide and 1/8 inches high except where it tapered to a sharp edge at the rear and bulged at the bottom as shown in Figure 4-43, to form a mounting boss for the extractor pin that secured it to the breechbolt. The boss was 9/32 inches high; it had a 3/32 inch diameter unthreaded hole for the extractor pin 2 5/64 inches from the front of the extractor. The extractor was made of spring steel and had a slightly-curved hook, or claw, 13/64 inches long, beveled on the front and curved on the back. This relatively sharp pointed bevel or incline on the front of the claw permitted the extractor hook to slide over the cartridge rim when the breechbolt was closed and withdraw the cartridge by its rim when the action was levered open.

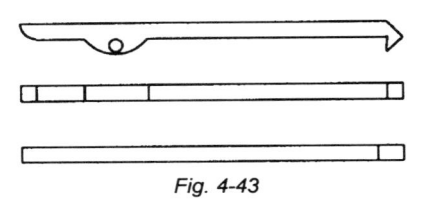

Fig. 4-43

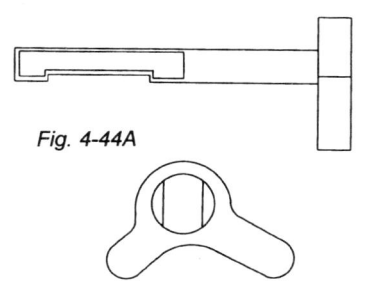

Fig. 4-44A

Ejector

The M1886 ejector assembly was a spring-actuated steel shaft 1 23/64 inches long, See Figure 4-44A. It had a head with two protrusions at the front which pushed the cartridge case from the receiver. The shaft was 9/64 inches in diameter, flat on both sides at the rear and milled out at the bottom rear for the lever and breechbolt pin which secured it in the action. The two tips on the head end were both 9/64 inches wide but were 7/32 inches and 5/32 inches long respectively.

The Models of 1886 and 1892

The ejector fit into a cutout in the face of the breechbolt and was pressed forward by a spring 31/64 inches long by 5/16 inches in diameter, Figure 4-44B. This spring had five coils of relatively thick 1/16 inch diameter spring steel wire. The springs were made of steel wire that was either square or round in cross-section with no apparent pattern of use.

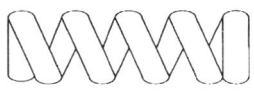

Fig. 4-44B

The ejector spring was secured on the ejector shaft by a tubular steel collar 3/16 inches long by 5/16 inches in outer diameter with walls 1/16 inches thick, Figure 4-44C. When the action was fully closed with a cartridge loaded, the rear of the cartridge case pressed the ejector head back into its cutout in the breechbolt face, compressing the spring. When the finger lever was pivoted downward to open the action and the breechbolt began to slide to the rear, the ejector spring pressed forward against the rear of the ejector, pushing the ejector head against the lower rear of the cartridge rim. When the front of the cartridge cleared the mouth of the chamber, the upward pressure of the spring bearing on the rear of the ejector head caused the cartridge to be expelled from the action through the opening in the top of the receiver.

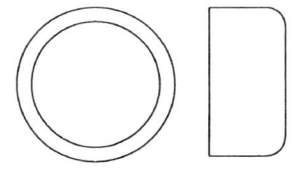

Fig. 4-44C

Winchester Lever Action Repeaters

Springs

Mainspring
The mainspring for the M1886 was identical to that used in the M1876. Like the Model 1876 mainspring, it lacked a mounting hole in its tang to secure it to the receiver. It slid into a slot milled into the upper tang screw stud on the inside surface of the lower tang. It was held laterally by the receiver walls and longitudinally by the main spring tension screw which allowed adjustments to the spring tension on the hammer to be made. See Figure 4-45.

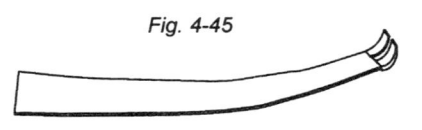

Fig. 4-45

The M1886 mainspring dimensions were 3 1/2 inches along the inner curve, 3 9/16 inches long along the outer curve, by 13/32 inches wide by 7/64 inches thick at the base end and 21/64 inches wide by 1/16 inches thick at the front or hook end.

NOTE: Mainsprings for the Models 1876 and 1886 are very hard to find and often, mainsprings manufactured for the Models 1866, 1873, 1892, and 1894 are substituted. They work fine if snugged up with the tension screw. They are not as strong as the M1876/86 mainspring and so do not allow the hammer to strike the firing pin with as much energy. Check any M1876 or M1886 spring which feels "soft." This can be corrected by adjusting pressure on the spring with the mainspring tension screw. Of course, a substitute spring does slightly reduce the value of an otherwise original M1886.

Carrier Spring and Screw
The carrier spring, on the underside of the upper tang, provided pressure on the carrier to hold it in the *up* position as the finger lever was lowered. Only when the finger lever was pulled past a certain point did the carrier spring release the pressure on the carrier and allow it to drop into position to receive a new cartridge from the magazine.

The Models of 1886 and 1892

The carrier spring was 1/2 inches wide at its widest point by 2 7/32 inches long. It was 9/64 inches thick at the base end and tapered to 1/16 inches thick at the front, or point, end. An 11/64 inch diameter unthreaded hole was drilled in the base for the carrier spring screw. See Figure 4-46.

Two types of carrier spring screws were used. Prior to circa serial #19,500, the **Type 1** carrier spring screw (A) was 15/32 inches long. Its head was 15/64 inches in diameter and 3/32 inches high. The screw shank was 3/8 inches long by 5/32 inches in diameter and had a 5/32 thread. The carrier spring screw was inserted from inside the upper tang, penetrated the carrier spring, and threaded into the upper tang, leaving the end of the screw shank flush with the outer surface of the top tang, just behind the forward tang sight mount screw hole.

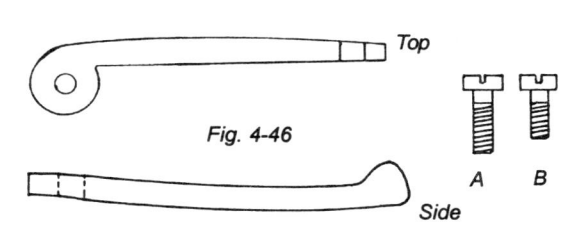

Between circa serial #19,500-23,500, the **Type 2** carrier spring screw (B) came into use, but was installed at the same time as the Type 1. The Type 2 was identical to the Type 1 except that it was only 3/8 inches long overall. After circa serial #23,500, the 3/8 inch long carrier spring screw was standardized. The Type 2 screw hole did not penetrate the upper tang and the screw shank was not visible. So, after circa serial #23,500, only two screw holes will be visible on the outer surface of the upper tang.

Winchester Lever Action Repeaters

ACTION

The M1886 action was designed by John M. and Matthew S. Browning and was the first Winchester lever action repeater to use the sliding vertical lock action. It was designed to handle the longer and more powerful black powder rounds like the .40-82, .45-70 and .45-90 Winchester Center Fire (WCF) cartridges. The action was normally quite smooth in operation. A sticky or rough action usually indicates one of two conditions: 1) a worn full cock notch that forces the hammer to ride on the rear of the breechbolt,

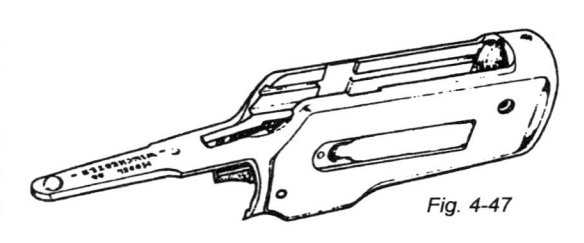

Fig. 4-47

or 2) a part broken or left out during reassembly. Either condition reduces the value of a M1886 rifle or carbine by at least twenty percent and more, depending on the scarcity of the part. See Figure 4-47.

Carrier

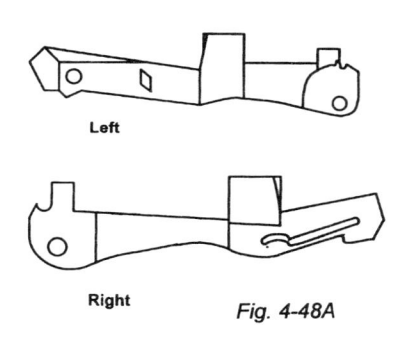

Left

Right

Fig. 4-48A

The M1886 carrier was a machined steel piece 4 11/16 inches long by 43/64 inches wide at its widest point. It had a 9/32 inch diameter unthreaded hole through the right side at the rear for the hammer screw. The carrier pivoted on the hammer screw. There was also a 2 3/64 inch long by 11/64 inch high slot for the carrier hook which pulled the next cartridge in line into the cartridge cradle on the front top surface of the carrier. The cradle was 7/16 inches wide by 2 19/32 inches long. A partial circle 39/64 inches in diameter was milled out at the rear of the cradle for the rim of the cartridge case. See Figure 4-48A.

The Models of 1886 and 1892

Carriers used on .50 caliber rifles and carbines were modified slightly to accommodate the larger diameter cartridge case (43/64 inches vs. 5/8 inches for all other calibers). The partial circle in the rear of the cradle was polished out an additional 3/64 of an inch larger to 21/32 inches.

NOTE: The design and movement of the carrier is one of two main distinguishing points between the M1886 and earlier model Winchester lever action rifles. When the breechbolt is closed and the finger lever is in the "up" position, a cam on the left front side of the bolt pushes the cartridge stop to the side and allows the next cartridge in the magazine tube to partially enter the receiver. The cartridge rim overrides the carrier hook claw because of pressure exerted on the bullet tip by the magazine follower. When the lever is lowered, the carrier hook draws the cartridge into the cartridge cradle on the carrier. The carrier is then pivoted upward by the carrier spring and raises the cartridge into line with the breechbolt. The upward movement of the carrier ends when the carrier stop stud on the left side of the carrier strikes the bottom edge of the cartridge stop. When the finger lever continues upward, the breechbolt moves forward. A cam on the bottom of the breechbolt slides into a slot in the top rear of the carrier, catching the cartridge rim and pushing the cartridge up the incline of the carrier cartridge cradle and into the chamber. The cartridge stop is pushed aside at the same time, which allows the next cartridge to partially enter the action to start the cycle all over again.

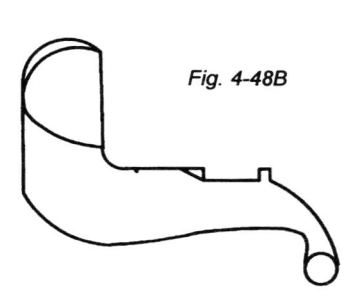

Fig. 4-48B

Carrier Hook

The carrier hook was a "J-shaped" piece of steel, 5/16 inches wide, 1 7/32 inches long and 1.0 inches high. It was mounted on the front of the carrier. See Figure 4-48B.

Winchester Lever Action Repeaters

To reduce the length of the magazine tube spring, John Browning designed the carrier hook to pull a cartridge from the magazine tube. The carrier hook for any caliber M1886 is very difficult to replace. If the carrier hook is broken or missing, the M1886 will appear to function when not loaded, although a bit roughly. But when loaded, cartridges will not feed, reducing the shooter to loading the rifle one cartridge at a time through the ejection port. The carrier hook is difficult to see in the open action without a strong light.

NOTE: The carrier hook is one of those parts which if broken or missing will reduce the value of a M1886 rifle or carbine by more than twenty percent.

Cartridge Guide

The cartridge guide was 3 11/64 inches long by 9/32 inches wide in the midsection. Only the width at the midpoint was significant. **Type 1** cartridge guides were 11/64 inches (0.175) inches wide for all calibers but the .50s. The **Type 2** .50 caliber cartridge guides were 20/1000's (0.173) inches thinner to accommodate the larger diameter .50 caliber cartridge cases. See Figure 4-49A.

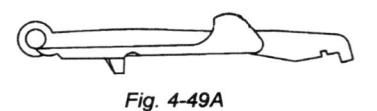

Fig. 4-49A

Cartridge Stop

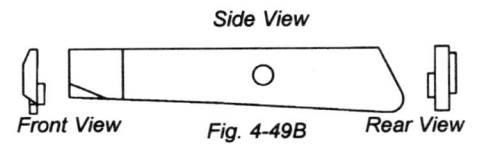

Only a single type of cartridge stop was produced. It was 2 5/16 inches long by 31/64 inches high at the highest point by 11/64 inches at the thickest point. It was attached to the receiver wall by the cartridge stop screw. The screw hole and screw were both threaded 3/16-36. See Figure 4-49B.

Side View
Front View   Fig. 4-49B   Rear View

The Models of 1886 and 1892

Loading Gate Assembly

Winchester's term was "spring cover," but modern collectors refer to it as the "loading gate." The loading gate for the M1886 was a radical departure from the one-piece spring steel gates made for previous models. All M1886 loading gate assemblies received the same finish as the receiver, except on special order. See Figure 4-50.

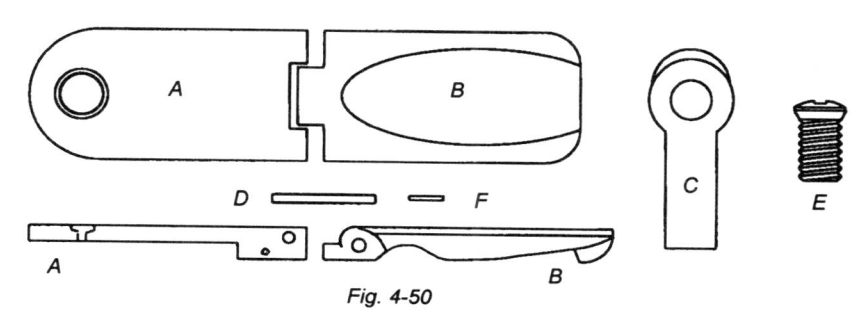

Fig. 4-50

The M1886 loading gate assembly consisted of six parts: A) base, B) leaf, C) leaf spring, D) leaf spring retaining pin, E) loading gate screw and F) loading gate stop pin. It could be separated from the receiver without disassembly. The entire assembly was 3 9/32 inches long by 11/16 inches wide.

The leaf, or forward portion of the loading gate was held closed by the leaf spring bearing on the cam on the inside surface of the leaf near the base. The base and leaf were pinned together and were hinged inward in the middle of the assembly. This apparently complex loading gate was required by the much longer cartridges the M1886 was designed to fire. If a one-piece spring steel loading gate had been used, as in previous models, the tip of the cartridge would have entered the mouth of the magazine tube before the rim passed into the receiver.

The front edge of the loading gate was milled off at a relatively sharp angle so it fit inside, and almost flush, with the receiver's surface when closed.

Winchester Lever Action Repeaters

NOTE: If the loading gate protrudes more than 1/16 inch above the receiver's surface examine it carefully for replaced or reproduction parts.

Loading Gate Base
The loading gate base (A) was the after end of the hinged assembly. The loading gate base was 11/16 inches wide by 1 23/32 inches long. It was milled on its underside with a cutout 1 19/32 inches long. The rounded end of the cutout was 7/16 inches in diameter and the slot for the body of the spring was 5/16 inches wide. The after end of the loading gate base was drilled with an unthreaded hole 13/64 inches in diameter, counter sunk to 5/16 inches in diameter for the loading gate screw.

The loading gate base was drilled at the front end with a vertical hole 3/32 inches in diameter through which the *loading gate leaf pin* passed to fasten the base and leaf together.

Loading Gate Leaf
The loading gate leaf (B) formed the front end of the two-piece loading gate. It was 11/16 inches wide by 1 53/64 inches long, including the spring cam. The loading gate leaf had a projection on its after edge that fitted into a corresponding cutout on the front edge of the loading gate base. A 3/32 inch diameter hole was drilled vertically through the projection for the *loading gate leaf pin* which fastened the leaf and base together and allowed the leaf to pivot inward. The loading gate leaf was case-hardened, therefore quite brittle, and tended to crack or chip. Examine this part carefully.

Loading Gate Spring
The loading gate spring (C) was 1 27/64 inches long. It was 7/16 inches in diameter at its rounded after end and tapered to 9/32 inches wide at the forward end. It varied from 1/16 to 1/64 inches thick.

The Models of 1886 and 1892

Loading Gate Pin
The loading gate pin (D) was 3/32 inches in diameter by 43/64 inches long and fitted into the 3/32 inch diameter holes on both the after end of the loading gate leaf and the forward end of the loading gate base.

Loading Gate Screw
The loading gate screw (E) had an oval head 1/4 inches in diameter by 1/16 inch high and 5/16 inches long overall. The shank was 3/16 inches in diameter by 1/4 inches long with a 3/16-36 thread pattern

Loading Gate Stop Pin
This pin (F) was called the "spring cover stop pin" by Winchester. It was press-fitted into a 1/16 inch diameter hole on the hinge stud of the loading gate cover base to prevent the leaf from being pushed beyond the center by the spring. The pin was 7/32 inches long and 1/16 inch in diameter.

NOTE: The M1886 loading gate assembly is nearly impossible to replace today, short of removing one from a "junk" gun. A malfunctioning loading gate, or one that protrudes from its cutout in the receiver, rates a considerable reduction in value.

Firing Pins
Three types of firing pins were used in the M1886, See Figure 4-51. **Type 1** was installed to circa serial #2,500. It was 4 9/16 inches long and 5/16 inches in diameter. The firing pin tip was 7/64 inches in diameter by 5/16 inches long. The M1886 Type 1 firing pin did not have the 15/32 inches cutout (arrow) on the bottom rear applied later to make it easier for the firing pin to override the hammer by pushing on the hammer face until it was fully cocked. The firing pin was retained in the firing pin tunnel in the breechbolt by the "lever and breechbolt pin."

The M1886 **Type 2** firing pin was installed from circa serial #2,500—110,000. After this point, it was installed intermittently with the M1886

Winchester Lever Action Repeaters

Type 3 with no pattern discernible. The Type 2 was identical to the Type 1 except that it had a cutout on the bottom rear to make it easier to push the hammer to the full cocked position. The cutout (arrow) was 15/32 inches long and 1/8 inches deep.

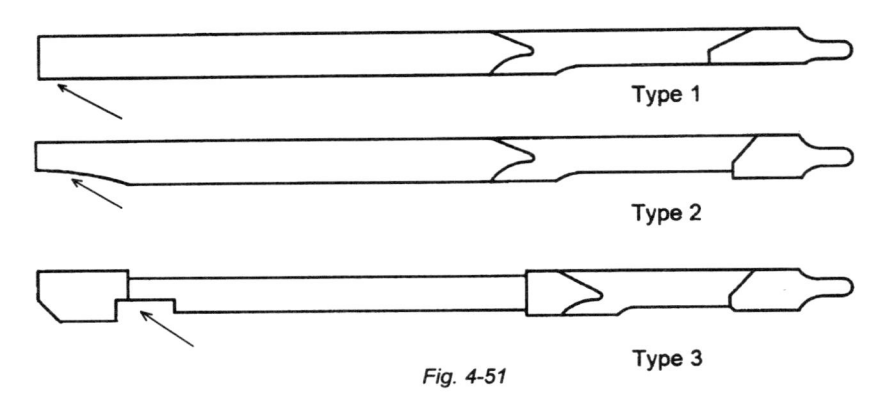

Fig. 4-51

The M1886 **Type 3** was installed beginning at circa serial #110,000 and used intermittently with the Type 2 until the end of production. It was identical in dimensions to the Type 2 but was now held in the breechbolt by a "firing pin stop pin." A corresponding elongated slot 15/64 inches long was cut crosswise on the bottom rear of the firing pin shaft (arrow) for the firing pin stop pin. The slot was long enough to allow the firing pin to withdraw so that the firing pin tip did not rest on the cartridge primer. This slot was centered 21/32 inches from the rear of the firing pin and was cut 3/32 inches deep.

The firing pin stop pin was 3/32 inches in diameter and 21/32 inches long and was press fitted into a hole in the breechbolt located 1 5/64 inches from the rear of the bolt to the center of the hole.

The Models of 1886 and 1892

FORENDS AND FOREARMS

Rifle Forends

Rifle forends for the M1886 were the same overall length—9 3/8 inches long—as for other lever action repeating models, but were larger in all other dimensions. The rifle forend was capped at the front with a forend tip held in place by two screws that threaded into a tenon held in a 3/8 inches wide dovetail cut into the bottom of the barrel. See Table 4-9 for dimensions and Figure 4-52.

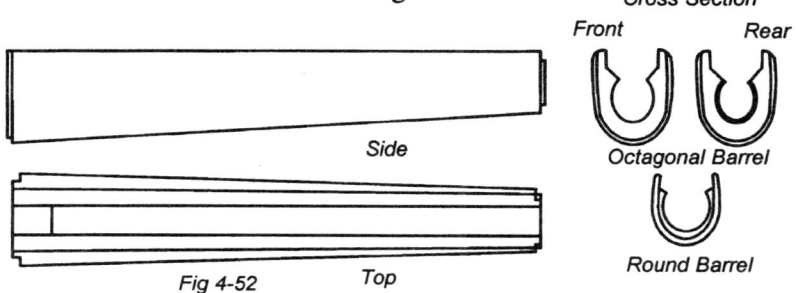

Fig 4-52

Forends for standard rifles were machined from select grade, straight grain walnut and were usually oil finished. While special finish forends were available on order, they are rare.

TABLE 4-9 RIFLE FOREND DIMENSIONS						
TYPE	LENGTH	WIDTH		HEIGHT	
		MUZZLE	RECEIVER	MUZZLE	RECEIVER
Standard	9 3/8 ± 1/8	1 7/32 ± 1/16	1 3/8 ± 1/16	1 11/32 ± 1/16	1 5/8 ± 1/16
Light-weight	9 3/8 ± 1/8	1 3/32 ± 1/16	1 3/8 ± 1/16	1 19/64 ± 1/16	1 5/8 ± 1/16

Takedown forends had the same specifications as their standard rifle counterparts, but can be identified by the "takedown extension cut-

Winchester Lever Action Repeaters

out" at the rear of the magazine tube tunnel which was 57/64 inches in diameter and extended forward into the magazine tube tunnel for 13/16 inches.

Carbine Forearms

Two types of carbine forearms were manufactured for the M1886 carbine. Early carbines were equipped with a long, musket-style forearm while later carbines were furnished with the conventional half-length carbine forearm.

Type 1 musket-style forearms were only made for the M1886 carbine from 1886 to early 1889 (between circa serial #s 1-30,000). The long "musket-style" forearm used on the early Model 1886 carbines were ostensibly made for consideration by the Canadian North West Mounted Police. They were similar to, but 1/8 to 1/4 inch shorter than the M1876 "musket-style" forearm installed on the NWMP carbines. They were 17 15/16 ± 1/16 inches long compared to 18 1/16 ± 1/16 inches long for the M1876 NWMP carbine forearm. See Figure 4-53.

The M1886 Type 1 musket-style forearm was 1 7/32 ± 1/32 inches wide at the breech end and 1 5/64 ± 1/32 inches wide at the muzzle end. The forearm was stepped at 12 3/16 inches from the front end for

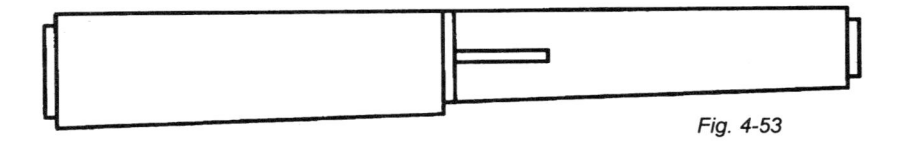

Fig. 4-53

the rear barrel band. A slot 1 23/64 inches long was milled into the side of this forearm and it ended in a 3/32 inches diameter hole into which the "foot" of the "L" on the band spring entered to secure the rear band. Variance was the result of the finishing process.

The M1886 musket style carbine forearm was held in place at the muzzle end by a single screw that passed through the forearm cap or

The Models of 1886 and 1892

tip and through a steel stud brazed to the bottom of the barrel three inches behind the muzzle. Because the hole in the stud tended to enlarge with wear, the Type 1 carbine forearm is almost always loose and can usually be moved back and forth as much as 1/16 of an inch. This looseness, while undesirable, is not considered a defect and will not reduce the collector value of the carbine.

A single barrel band held the Type 1 forearm to the barrel. It was in turn held in place by a barrel band spring. See page 80.

Type 2 carbine forearms were used after the Type 1 musket style forearms were discontinued at circa serial #30,000. They were quite similar in appearance to those used on earlier models but were different in all dimensions. The M1886 Type 2 carbine forearm was 9 7/8 inches long as compared to 9 1/8 inches long for other models. It was 1 25/64 ± 1/16 inches wide at the receiver end, 1 15/64 ± 1/16 inches wide just behind the rear barrel band, 1 9/64 ± 3/64 inches wide immediately in front of the rear barrel band and 1 3/64 ± 1/32 inches wide at the front of the forearm. See Figure 4-54.

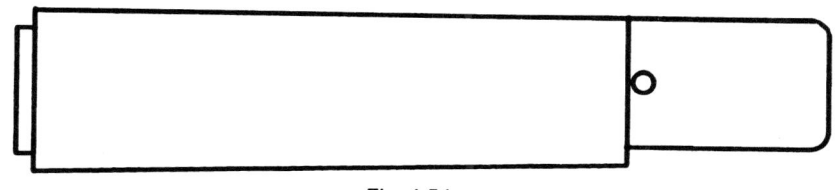

Fig. 4-54

Type 2 carbine forearms were 1 41/64 ± 1/16 inches high at the receiver end, 1 23/64 ± 1/16 inches high just behind the rear barrel band, 1 9/32 ± 3/64 inches high immediately in front of the rear barrel band and the height tapered slightly both top and bottom to 1 37/64 ± 1/16 inches at the extreme front of the forearm.

Winchester Lever Action Repeaters

The rear barrel band was placed 1/2 inches farther forward on the M1886 Type 2 forearm than on any other model and was positioned 7 5/32 ± 1/16 inches ahead of the receiver face. Although the rear band was about half an inch farther forward on the M1886 carbine, only 1/4 inch more wood showed in front of the band than on other models.

Rifle Forend Tips

The standard rifle forend tip was 1 13/64 inches wide by 1 1/16 ± 1/64 inches long and the magazine tube hole was 49/64 inches in diameter for all calibers. The upper part of the magazine tube opening was open for 7/32 inches.

NOTE: The magazine tube hole, like the magazine inner and outer diameters, was the same for all calibers.

NOTE: On takedown models, the magazine tube hole was slightly larger at 25/32 inches in diameter to make it easier to unscrew the magazine tube without scratching its finish.

At the rear of the forend tip, a collar was milled around the interior 7/32 inches deep which fitted into a corresponding cutout on the front edge of the forend. The cutout on the front of the forend was 1/8 inches for both the standard and lightweight forend.

There were two variations of the standard rifle forend tip (see Figure 4-55): 1) round barrel and 2) octagon barrel. Round barrels do fit into octagon forend tips but not vice-versa.

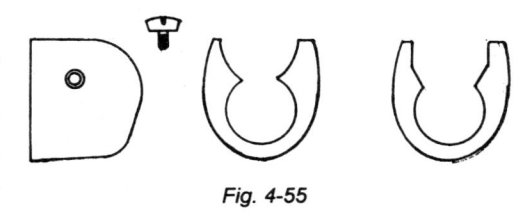

Fig. 4-55

The round barrel forend tip will not allow the octagon barrel to "sit" far enough down for the screws to be installed in the tenon. The octagon tip, however, will, but will show visible gaps on either side of the barrel. Since either forend tip can be altered to accommodate the other barrel, examine them carefully for signs of cutting and filling.

The Models of 1886 and 1892

Rifle forend tips were color case hardened to circa serial #122,000; after, they were blued. When faded with age and exposure to the sun, it was often difficult to determine if a forend tip was color case hardened or blued.

NOTE: If a rifle forend tip is dark, or blued, and was made before circa serial #122,000 look carefully for signs of rebluing—pits that have been polished out or screw holes with dished edges.

Forend tips for M1886 rifles with heavy or extra heavy barrels were made wider to match the width of the barrel. The cutout was also wider.

Dimensions for the forend tips installed on lightweight and extra lightweight rifles differed from the standard rifle forend tip. The forend tip for the lightweight and extra lightweight barrel with the rapid taper was 1 3/64 inches long overall and had a magazine tube opening 23/32 inches in diameter. But it was narrower at 1 3/32 inches wide than the standard rifle forend tip and the magazine tube hole made a complete circle (these barrels were made only in the round configuration. See Figure 4-56.

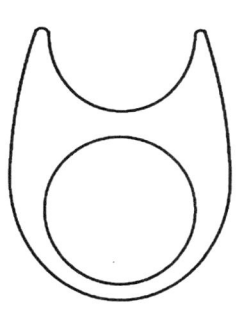

Fig. 4-56

All M1886 forend tips had a countersunk, unthreaded hole on each side, 9/64 inches in diameter for the forend tip screws which secured it to the forend tip tenon.

Carbine Forearm Tips

The **Type 1** Musket-style carbine forearm was secured by a forearm tip. It was 1 7/16 inches long by 1 3/32 inches wide by 1 3/16 inches high. See Figure 4-57.

Winchester Lever Action Repeaters

The tip was held in place by a single screw with an unbeveled head 1/4 inches in diameter and 5/64 inches high. The screw was 1 3/32 inches long overall; the shank was 3/16 inches in diameter and was threaded 3/16-36 for a distance of 19/64 inches from the end.

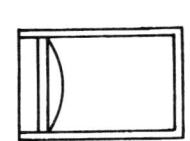

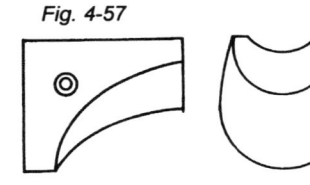

Fig. 4-57

A single screw passed through the tip from the right side, through a stud brazed to the bottom of the barrel, and screwed into a threaded hole in the left side of the forearm tip. The end of the screw was flush with the outer surface of the forearm tip.

NOTE: The magazine end plug used with the Type 1 carbine forearm was held in place only by the forend tip and was not secured by a screw. Use care when disassembling as the magazine end plug is under tension from the magazine spring.

M1886 carbines fitted with the Type 2 carbine forearm did not use a forearm tip.

Forend Tip Tenon
There were two distinct sizes of forend tip tenons installed on M1886 rifles. **Type 1** was used on standard weight, heavy weight or extra heavy weight barrels. It was 29/32 inches long and 3/8 inches wide. See Figure 4-58.

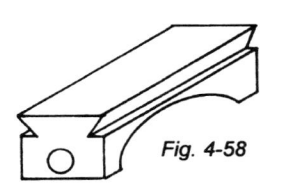

Fig. 4-58

The **Type 2** forend tip tenon was installed on M1886 rifle barrels with the lightweight and extra lightweight rapid taper barrels which required the Type 2 narrow forend tip. The Type 2 forend tip tenon was similar to the Type 1 but was only 51/64 inches long by 3/8 inches wide. It was beveled at the front to ease installation of the narrow forend tip.

The Models of 1886 and 1892

The M1886 Type 2 forend tip tenon was identical to that installed on all variations of the Model 71. See Figure 4-59.

Both the Type 1 and the Type 2 forend tip tenons were press-fitted into a 3/8 inch wide dovetail cut across the bottom of the barrel. Both the Type 1 and Type 2 tenons had concave surface to fit the contour of the magazine tube. They were also drilled through and threaded 6-48 on both sides to accept the two forend tip screws.

Forend Tip Screws

Two screws were used to hold the forend tip to the forend tip tenon. They entered from either side of the forend tip. They were 1/4 inch long and had 6-48 threads.

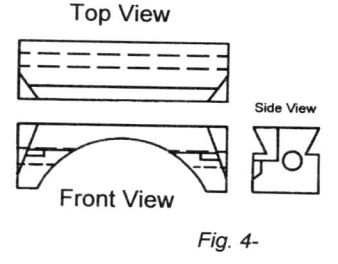

Fig. 4-

These same screws were used on all lever action repeating rifles except the M1895. These same screws were also used on "Pre-1964" M1894 rifles.

Winchester Lever Action Repeaters

BARRELS

As in predecessor models, the round barrel was standard in the M1886 and the octagon barrel was a modest extra-cost option, see Figure 4-60. In spite of this company policy, the octagon barrel continued to prove more popular. As a consequence, M1886 rifles with round barrels are today quite a bit rarer although paradoxically, the octagon is more popular with collectors and thus commands a premium. See also Table 4-10 for dimensions.

Fig. 4-60

TABLE 4-10 MODEL 1886 STANDARD BARREL LENGTHS	
Standard Barrel Length to circa serial #125,000	26 inches
Standard Barrel Length after circa serial #125,000	24 inches
Special Order Lightweight Barrel Length circa serial #115,000 +	24 inches
.33 Winchester Center Fire Barrel, circa serial #128,000	24 inches
Special Order Extra Lightweight Barrel Length, circa serial #25,000	22 inches
Extra Lightweight 45-70 Barrel Length	22 inches
Carbine Barrel Length	22 inches

Winchester barrels were notorious for their variation in length. The M1886 barrel will invariably be 1/16 to 1/8 inch shorter than specified. Measure all Winchester barrels from the muzzle to the rear of the chamber. See Table 4-11.

The Models of 1886 and 1892

TABLE 4-11
WINCHESTER MODEL 1886 OTHER BARREL DIMENSIONS

Type	Configur-ation	Cross Section	Diameter at Breech (inches)	Diameter at Muzzle (inches)
Rifle	Standard	Round	7/8 ± 1/16	11/16 ± 1/16
		Octagon	27/32 ± 1/16	45/64 ± 1/16
	Rapid Taper	Round/Octagon	15/16 ± 1/16	41/64 ± 1/16
	Heavy	Round	31/32 ± 5/64	55/64 ± 5/64
		Octagon	1 7/64 ± 3/32	29/32 ± 5/64
	Extra Heavy	Round/Octagon	1 3/16 ± 3/32	1 ± 3/32
	Lightweight	Round	7/8 ± 1/16	41/64 ± 1/32
	Extra Lightweight	Round	7/8 ± 1/16	41/64 ± 1/32
Carbine	Standard	Round	31/32 ± 3/64	11/16 ± 1/32

Shorter or longer than standard barrel lengths were available on special order in 2 inch increments from 20 to 36 inches. Winchester would even provide a barrel in an odd length if the customer insisted. There are recorded barrel lengths in odd number increments; two in particular were unique at 19 and 21 inches respectively. Winchester even made extremely rare 14 1/2 inch barrel M1886s in .45-70 caliber as line-throwing guns for the U.S. Coast Guard.

Winchester Lever Action Repeaters

NOTE: Special length barrels in the Model 1886, particularly in longer-than-standard-lengths, were rarer than in any previous models. As early as circa serial #25,000, the records show rare, shorter-than-standard-length rifles with 22 and 24 inch barrels on special order. These may have been the precursors of the lightweight and extra-lightweight variations introduced at circa serial #115,000. The standard Model 1886 rifle, depending on caliber, weighed in, when fully loaded, at around eight pounds which made the lighter variations quite desirable. Lightweight and extra lightweight rifles were offered in .33 W.C.F. and .45-70 only. Earlier special order guns with lighter, shorter barrels, although appearing identical to the standard lightweight and extra lightweight arms, were usually found in other calibers. It is the author's opinion that even when these earlier special order rifles with lighter barrels were chambered for the .45-70 cartridge, it was only coincidental.

NOTE: M1886 rifle variations with rapid taper octagon barrels, all in 33 W.C.F. or 45-70 calibers, were considered by Winchester as special order guns.

M1886 rifles and, very rarely, carbines, which used the Type 1 Magazine End Plug had a slot 25/64 inches wide by 5/64 inches long cut 1/8 inches behind the muzzle on the bottom of the barrel to accept the magazine tube end plug lip that rotated into the slot.

M1886 rifles and carbines which used the Type 2 and 5 Magazine Tube End Caps had a blind hole 1/8 inches in diameter, 3/32 inches deep drilled in the underside of the barrel, 5/8 inches behind the muzzle (to the center of the hole) which received the blunt, unthreaded end of the long 25/32 inch magazine end plug screw.

The top rear inside chamber surface on all .50 caliber barrels was polished to facilitate chambering the larger diameter .50 caliber cartridge. Any .50 caliber barrel that does not show this polish should be considered suspect regarding its factory-original caliber.

The Models of 1886 and 1892

NOTE: When authenticating a .50 caliber barrel, check for the polished chamber, and also for the milled-out area on the right side of the finger lever just ahead of the carrier hook that allowed the loading gate to open farther inward. Also check the cartridge cradle for the larger (21/32 inches) partial circle cut to accommodate the larger diameter cartridge, and the caliber markings on the underside of the barrel beneath the forearm or forend. See also Appendix D.

M1886 special order "half round/half octagon" barrels will show the transition from octagon to round as a smooth, gradual slope of about sixty degrees, somewhat steeper than on other lever action repeating models. See Figure 4-61.

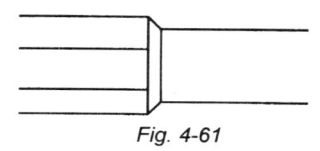

Fig. 4-61

Properly speaking, these barrels were not half round/half octagon as the transition occurred just ahead of the forend—usually ten inches ahead of the receiver face. But the location of the transition zone from octagon to round could vary between 3/16 to 2 1/8 inches ahead of the forend tip, more than in any other lever action repeating model, as shown in Table 4-12.

TABLE 4-12	
MODEL 1886 HALF OCTAGON/HALF ROUND TRANSITION MEASUREMENTS	
TYPE OF RIFLE	DISTANCE AHEAD OF FOREND TIP (INCHES)
Full Length Magazine Rifles	1/4 to 3/4
Button Magazine Rifles	3/16 to 9/16
Fractional Length Magazines	3/4 to 2 1/8

Some half round/half octagon barrels will show a narrow circular groove between the two sections. This may have been a manufacturing artifact as the transition from octagon to round was cut manually on a lathe.

Winchester Lever Action Repeaters

Takedown barrels were machined with interrupted threads that formed the top and bottom of an arc. The threads were cut 20 to the inch. The barrel was turned 90 degrees and slipped into the receiver socket, then turned back 90 degrees to engage the threads. The extractor cutout passed only through the last four interrupted threads. See Figure 4-62.

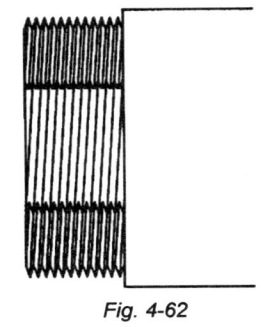

Barrels installed on takedown rifles to circa serial #110,000 and which employed the Type 1 takedown magazine end cap and lever will show a slot or groove milled in the underside of the barrel approximately 1/2 inch long and 5/32 inches wide.

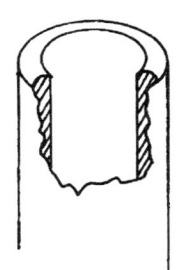

Fig. 4-62

Barrel Crown
Carbine barrels were crowned but rifle barrels were not unless the customer requested it on special order. The carbine crown is 1/64 inch. See Figure 4-63.

Fig. 4-63

Dovetails
Dovetails on all M1886 rifle barrels were 3/8 inches wide, as on all other lever action repeater models with the exception of the 1/2 inch long dovetails for the rear sight on Model 1866 carbines to circa serial #15,500. See Figure 4-64.

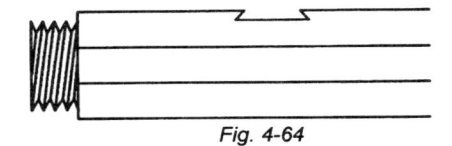

Fig. 4-64

Dovetails were cut on all barrels for the rear sight. Front sight dovetails were cut only on standard, heavy and extra-heavy rifle barrels 3/4 ± 1/32 inches behind the muzzle. Front sight bases on all other barrels were soldered on. Table 4-13 provides the location of all rear sight dovetails.

The Models of 1886 and 1892

TABLE 4-13 M1886 BARREL DOVETAIL CUTS FOR REAR SIGHT BASES (INCHES)		
TYPE OF BARREL	**REAR SIGHT AHEAD OF RECEIVER FACE**	**FRONT SIGHT BEHIND MUZZLE**
Standard Rifle Barrels, Round or Octagon	4 3/4 Approximately*	3/4 ± 1/32
Lightweight Barrels	3 3/4 Approximately	15/32**
Extra Lightweight Barrels	3 3/4 Approximately	15/32**
Carbine Barrels, Type 1 Forearm	2 to 2 1/8	23/32 Approximately
Carbine Barrels, Type 2 Forearm	2 1/2 ± 1/16	5/8 ± 1/32**
Carbines with "long ladder" rear sight	2 1/2 ± 1/16	Depending on Forearm Type

* Exact placement apparently depended on the assembler.
** Front sight bases were not held in a dovetail but were soldered to the barrel.

The M1886 carbine Type 1 forearm was not held with a tenon dovetailed to the barrel. The early long forearm tip was secured to a stud or tang on the bottom of the barrel. See Figure 4-65.

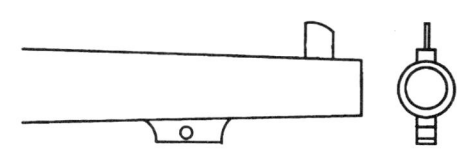

Fig. 4-65

The Type 2 carbine forearm was secured with a barrel band held in place by a screw that penetrated from left to right.

Winchester Lever Action Repeaters

The magazine tube ring slot was, strictly speaking, not a dovetail as it was milled in the shape of an ellipse. It was 53/64 inches long. See Figure 4-66.

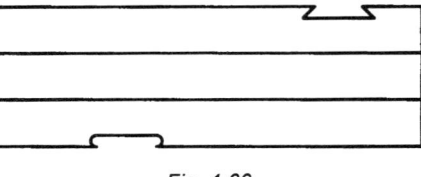

Fig. 4-66

Barrel Markings
Barrel Address Markings—Rifle
Barrel address markings for the Model 1886 were located on the top of the barrel, ahead of the rear sight dovetail on rifles, and between the rear sight dovetail and the rear barrel band on carbines.

Octagon Barrels—From the start of production to circa serial #60,000, the address markings found on the Model 1886 *octagon* barrel, read from muzzle to breech in block letters without serifs:

—MANUFACTURED BY THE—
—WINCHESTER REPEATING ARMS CO. NEW HAVEN, CONN. U.S.A.—

The top line was 1 7/32 inches long, including the dashes; the bottom line was 3 7/32 inches long, including the dashes. There was a minute difference in the length of the dashes in that those preceding were 9/64 inches long while the rear dashes were only 1/8 inches long. This was probably a minor error in the making of the die and does not signify a change in the markings. The letters in both lines were 5/64 inches high.

Round Barrels—From the start of production to circa serial #60,000, address markings on *round* barrels read from muzzle to breech in block letters without serifs:

—< MANUFACTURED BY THE >—
—< WINCHESTER REPEATING ARMS CO. NEW HAVEN CONN. U.S.A. >—

The Models of 1886 and 1892

Notice that in these markings the dashes have decorative arrow feathers, there was no period or comma after the word "HAVEN" and the letters were considerably larger than on the octagon barrel at 3/32 inches high. The top line was 1 27/32 inches long including arrows, and the bottom line was 4 13/32 inches long, also including the arrows. The arrows were not of uniform length. The preceding arrow, top line was 7/32 inches long while the rear top arrow was 3/16 inches long. The bottom line arrows, preceding and rear were 17/64 inches long.

From circa serial #60,000-140,000, the dash marks begin to appear intermittently on the top line only while the rest of the markings remains the same. When the dashes were absent, the line length was reduced to 1 1/2 inches.

At circa serial #140,000, the address marking on both octagon and round barrels was changed to read:

MANUFACTURED BY THE WINCHESTER REPEATING ARMS CO.
NEW HAVEN CONN. U.S.A. PAT. OCT. 14 1884. JAN. 20. 1885

These markings were in block letters without serifs 3/32 inches high. The top line was 3 17/32 inches long and the lower line 3 3/8 inches long. As with the early round barrel marking, there was no period or comma after the word "HAVEN" or after the number "14" in the patent date. Periods were used in place of commas (either that or the die wore sufficiently for the comma to give the appearance of a period).

Barrel Address Markings-Carbine
The carbine barrel address remained unchanged throughout M1886 carbine production. It read from muzzle to breech in block letters without serifs 5/64 inches high:

—MANUFACTURED BY THE—
—WINCHESTER REPEATING ARMS CO. NEW HAVEN, CONN. U.S.A.—

Winchester Lever Action Repeaters

The top line was 1 7/32 inches long, including the dashes; the bottom line was 3 7/32 inches long, including the dashes. There was a minute difference in the length of the dashes in that the preceding ones were 9/64 inches long while the rear dashes were only 1/8 inches long. A coma followed the word "Haven,".

Nickel Steel Barrel Markings
Barrels made of nickel steel were sometimes installed on the M1886 rifle and carbine after 1895 (circa serial #95,000) when these barrels were first introduced. They were marked on the left side approximately 1 3/16 inches in front of the receiver:

NICKEL STEEL BARREL
ESPECIALLY FOR SMOKELESS POWDER

Both lines were in block letters without serifs, 3/64 inches high. The top line was 1 5/32 inches long and the bottom line was 1 11/16 inches long.

After circa serial #150,000, this marking was dropped and nickel steel barrels were marked:

NICKEL STEEL

The line was 31/32 inches long in block letters 1/4 inches high, and without serifs.

All lightweight and extra-lightweight barrels were made of nickel steel and so marked. These barrels will show either of the above markings, depending on when they were made. Lightweight and extra-lightweight barrels were introduced at circa serial #115,000.

Some of the very last Model 1886s which were made up out of parts on hand in the late 1920's and early 1930s without nickel steel barrels

The Models of 1886 and 1892

may be marked "**WINCHESTER PROOF STEEL**" on the barrel. Also some of the last guns will be marked "**MADE IN U.S.A.**" This last marking may be found on either side of the barrel. The markings were 11/64 and 3/4 inches long with letters 5/64 and 3/32 inches high, respectively.

Some of these late barrels will show the model marking, "**MODEL 1886**", on the barrel rather than on the upper tang. It was placed on the barrel in case they were exported to England which required the year of introduction be stamped where it was easily visible to customs inspectors.

Winchester Proof Mark

The Winchester proof mark, a "**W**" and "**P**" inside an oval, first appeared on M1886 rifles and carbines at circa serial number 120,000. All made after circa serial number 135,000 (1905) should show the Winchester proof mark. The "**WP**" indicated that the firearm was "Viewed and Passed."

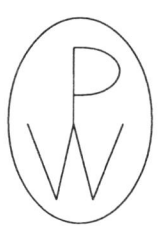

On factory repairs or alterations accomplished after circa 1900, the Winchester proof mark will almost always have been stamped on the barrel.

Caliber Markings

The caliber markings were located at the rear of the barrel, just behind the rear sight and again, on the bottom of the barrel under the forearm or forend. They were applied by a roll-stamp and so should have the same appearance at the edges and in the trough of the numbers as the barrel address. Examine caliber markings under strong magnification to make certain they were not engraved (uneven lines and erratic cuts).

When a caliber change was requested, the Winchester factory tended to simply change barrels rather than rebore and restraighten the original one. The new caliber was always roll-stamped on the new barrel.

Winchester Lever Action Repeaters

Other Markings
A variety of different markings are often found on the bottom of the barrel under the forearm or forend. These are mostly proof marks of one kind or another. "NS" indicates a barrel of nickel steel. "G" or other single initials are the barrel maker's initial. Various other markings will also be seen whose significance is unknown, including a bisected triangle and "heart-shaped" symbol.

The Problem of Barrel Changes
Barrels were changed for a variety of reasons; i.e., to replace one worn out by shooting or corrosion, to alter the barrel's length or form or to change calibers. For instance, a M1886 rifle with a "shorter than standard 24-inch barrel" made before that length became standard at circa serial #125,000, may well have had its barrel changed. To determine if the change was made at the Winchester factory, first check to see if the barrel has the Winchester proof mark stamped near the breech end. If it does, the change was made after 1900. If not, it was either made before 1900 or the work is non-factory. Obtaining a factory letter may be helpful. (See Appendix H). But factory records for lever action repeating firearms tend to be vague, particularly concerning factory-accomplished repairs or changes. If the information in the factory letter does not support the features of your rifle or carbine, you must then decide for yourself if the work was performed at Winchester, or by another source. But keep in mind that even if you convince yourself, you may not convince a future purchaser.

NOTE: When a M1886's caliber is changed by rechambering the original barrel, the person changing it may not be aware of, interested in, or may just overlook changing the caliber marking on the bottom of the barrel. If you suspect the caliber has been changed, check here first. An after-market caliber change by anyone other than the Winchester factory is considered a major alteration and renders the gun considerably less desirable as a collector's item. If the caliber was changed at the factory, the caliber markings will also be changed and this will not detract from the gun's collectible value.

The Models of 1886 and 1892

Rear Barrel Bands

Rear barrel bands were used only on the carbine. Two types were used depending on the forearm installed. All rear barrel bands were blued.

To circa serial #30,000, the **Type 1** carbine rear barrel band was used with the Type 1 musket-style forearm. The carbine rear barrel band was 1 55/64 inches high, 1/2 inches long and 7/64 inches thick. Like its predecessor, it employed a "band spring" rather than screws to hold it in place. See Figure 4-67 and 4-69.

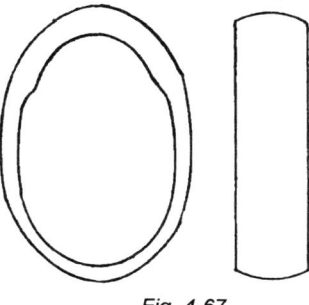

Fig. 4-67

After circa serial #30,000, the M1886 **Type 2** rear barrel band was used with the Type 2 carbine forearm. The Type 2 rear barrel band was held in place with a single screw that passed through the left side, then through a groove cut in the both the barrel and the magazine and threaded into the right side of the rear barrel band. The M1886 rear barrel band was similar to the rear barrel band used on the later M1892 and M1894, but it will not interchange as it was considerably larger and held in place by a longer screw. See Figure 4-68.

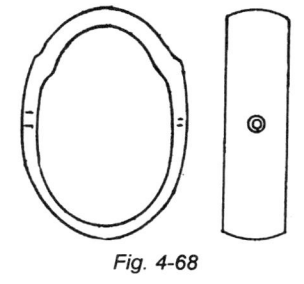

The **Type 2** rear barrel band was 1/2 inches long, 1 15/16 ± 1/32 inches high overall, 1 11/32 ± 1/32 inches across at its widest point and 7/64 inches thick. The inside dimensions of the Type 2 rear barrel band were 1 3/4 ± 1/32 inches high by 27/32 inches wide at the shoulders and 1 3/16 inches wide at its widest inside point (inside widths were ± 1/32 inches, also).

Fig. 4-68

Winchester Lever Action Repeaters

The **Type 2** rear barrel band was drilled on both sides of the band for the retaining screw. The left hole was 1/8 inches in diameter and countersunk to 7/32 inches in diameter. The right hole was 7/64 inches in diameter and threaded 4-56.

Rear Barrel Band Spring
The rear barrel band spring used only with the Type 1 rear barrel band, was shaped like an "L", see Figure 4-69. The longer stroke was 1 35/64 inches long by 11/64 inches wide. The outer surface had a concave curve 7/32 inches from the end which served to keep the band in place. The horizontal stroke was 1 1/16 inches long and 3/32 inches in diameter.

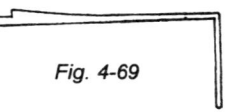

Fig. 4-69

Rear Barrel Band Screw
The M1886 rear barrel band screw was 1 11/32 inches long. The shank was 7/64 inches in diameter and threaded 4-56 for 17/64 inches of its length at the end. The head was 13/64 inches in diameter by 1/16 inches high.

Sling Hooks or Eyes
Sling hooks, also referred to as "sling eyes," on the M1886 rifle or carbine were a special order item. Two different types were used for the front and back.

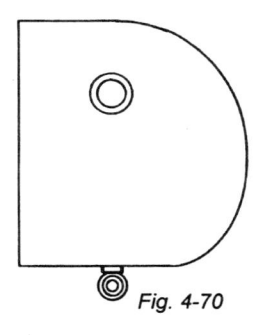

Fig. 4-70

The same **front** sling hook was mounted on the forend tip of standard, lightweight or extra lightweight rifles. The front sling hook had an eye mounted on a short shaft. The shaft penetrated a hole drilled in the forend tip or carbine barrel band and was peened flat to hold it in place. It was not intended to swivel or turn and does so only if loose in its mount. See Figure 4-70.

The Models of 1886 and 1892

The same front sling hook was also mounted on the carbine front barrel band. In both cases, the dimensions were identical. See Figure 4-71. The front sling eye had an outside diameter of 23/64 inches and an inside diameter of 13/64 inches. The flange was 5/16 inches in diameter and 1/32 inches high. The hole was countersunk on both sides to 19/64 inches in diameter. The front sling eye stud was 5/32 inches long and was inserted into the rifle's forend tip or the carbine's rear barrel band through a 9/64 inch diameter hole which was not counterbored or countersunk. The protruding end was crushed to retain the sling eye in place.

The **rear** sling eye screwed into the stock 4 ± 1/2 inches ahead of the toe (some original sling hooks were installed at 2 1/2 and 5 1/2 inches ahead of the toe), centered from side to side.

Fig. 4-71A

The eye was 3/8 inches in diameter and the hole in the eye was 13/64 inches, countersunk on both sides to 19/64 inches. The eye was mounted on a base or flange 21/64 inches in diameter and 1/32 inches high. The hole for the eye was offset to the top. The shank was straight, 7/32 inches in diameter by 11/16 inches long, and had 10 threads to the inch. Only the top 3/64 inches of the shank was unthreaded. The tip was rounded. See Figure 4-71B.

Fig. 4-71B

NOTE: Check any sling hooks screwed into a stock carefully. Winchester used a jig to install them so that they were exactly centered and the sling hook shank was straight. Aftermarket sling hooks are rarely installed using a jig and will usually be off-center and slant right or left.

Winchester Lever Action Repeaters

Front Barrel Band—Carbine

The M1886 front barrel band was installed only on those carbines equipped with the Type 2 forearm. It was made of steel, was 7/64 inches thick and blued. It was shaped like a figure eight with the lower half wider than the upper half. The M1886 front barrel band was larger than that used on any other model and so was not interchangeable. See Figure 4-72.

The M1886 carbine front band exterior dimensions were 1 9/16 inches high, 55/64 inches wide and 15/32 inches long from front to rear edges. edges. The interior dimensions were: barrel opening, 11/16 inches in diameter; magazine tube opening, 3/4 inches in diameter.

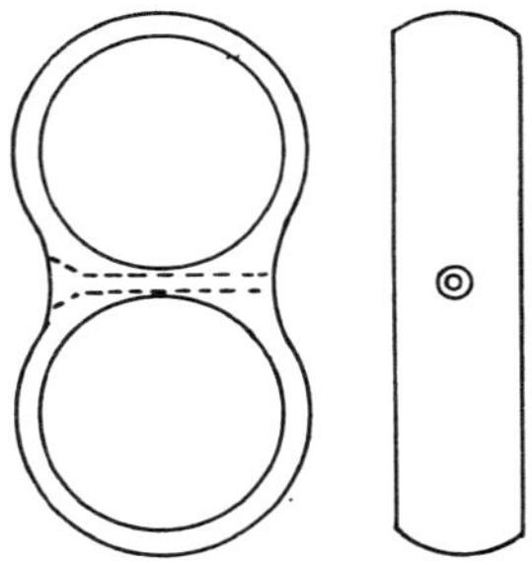

The front barrel band was drilled for the front barrel band screw. The hole on the left side was 1/8 inches in diameter and countersunk to 7/32 inches. On the right side, it was 7/64 inches in diameter and threaded 4-56.

The M1886 carbine barrel band was *always* installed *behind* the front sight. This differs from other models where the front barrel band was always installed *ahead* of the front sight, except for the late M1892 and M1894 carbines equipped with the ramp front sight.

Fig. 4-72

Front Barrel Band Screw

The front barrel band screw had a slotted oval head and was 13/16 inches long overall. The shank was 7/64 inches in diameter and threaded 4-56 for 17/64 inches of its length.

The Models of 1886 and 1892

Magazine Tubes

The M1886 magazine tube was unique to that model and cannot be substituted for that of any other model. The same magazine tube was used for all calibers of the M1886 lever actions and any caliber M1886 magazine tube can be interchanged freely for any other caliber M1886 magazine tube.

All M1886 magazine tubes were made from sheet steel 3/64 inches thick, rolled into a tube slightly shorter than the barrel length (see Table 4-14). The outer diameter was 47/64 inches and the inner diameter 41/64 inches. The tube ends were not welded or brazed together.

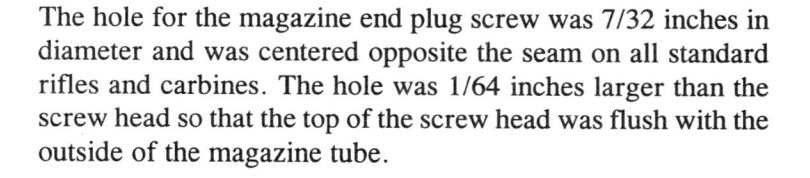

The hole for the magazine end plug screw was 7/32 inches in diameter and was centered opposite the seam on all standard rifles and carbines. The hole was 1/64 inches larger than the screw head so that the top of the screw head was flush with the outside of the magazine tube.

When the magazine tube was properly installed on the rifle or carbine, the magazine end plug screw hole was at the 6 o'clock position and the magazine tube seam 12 o'clock position. There were three types of M1886 magazine tubes.

The **Type 1** magazine tube (see Fig. 4-73A) was held in place by a pin through the magazine tube ring on rifles, or barrel band screws that penetrated the front and rear barrel bands on carbines. These methods proved unsatisfactory with the large calibers because of the recoil they produced. The Type 1 was used from the start of production to circa serial # 110,000.

Fig. 4-73A

Starting at circa serial #110,000, the **Type 2** magazine tube (see Figure 4-73B) was threaded at the rear and screwed into the receiver. The magazine tube threads were cut 40 to the inch and were quite

Winchester Lever Action Repeaters

TABLE 4-14
M1886 MAGAZINE TUBE LENGTHS
(INCHES)

BARREL LENGTH	NOMINAL LENGTH	ACTUAL LENGTH
22 (carbine)	21 1/4	21 1/16 to 21 1/4
22 (Light and Extra Light Weight)	21 1/4	21 1/16 to 21 1/4
24	23 1/2	23 1/4 to 23 1/2
26	25 1/8	24 15/16 to 25 1/8

shallow. As a result, the magazine tubes often rusted into the receiver, making them difficult to remove. Despite this drawback, magazine tubes continued to be threaded to the end of production, and on the continuation Model 71 as well.

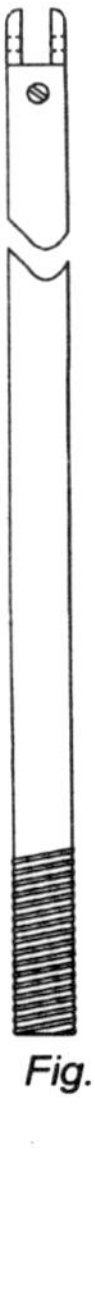

The **Type 3** magazine tube (see Figure 4-73C) installed on the M1886 takedown rifle had the same dimensions as the standard rifle magazine tube, but were threaded on the receiver end from the beginning of production. They were also cut and drilled at the muzzle end for installation of the takedown lever, cap assembly and cap assembly screw. This last screw was identical to the short magazine end plug screw.

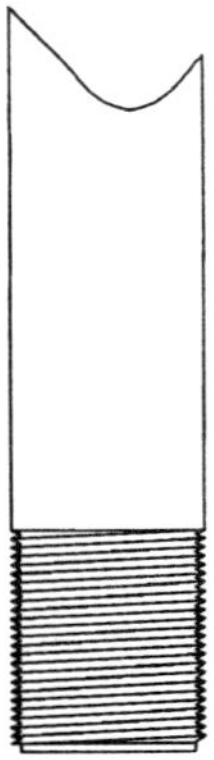

Fig. 4-73B

NOTE: Winchester called these items the magazine lever and plug assembly, and the magazine lever screw.

The takedown magazine tube was machined at the receiver end with a relatively coarse 11 threads per inch. The threads were cut 1/64 inches deep by 1/16 inches wide. The tube was threaded a distance of 1 9/16 inches.

Fig. 4-73C

The Models of 1886 and 1892

NOTE: Reproductions observed all have 12 threads. All original Winchester magazine tubes were seamed while most reproductions are made from seamless tubing.

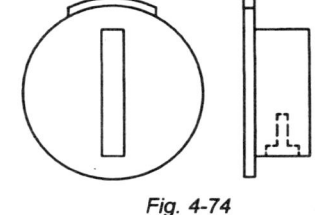

Fig. 4-74

The magazine end plug screw hole on takedown rifle magazines was drilled at the 6 o'clock position with the tube installed in the rifle with the seam at the 1:30 position. When disassembling the M1886 takedown rifle, the owner had to grasp the takedown lever firmly in one hand, and twist the magazine tube counterclockwise to unscrew it from the takedown extension. As the seam was the weakest part of the magazine tube, the factory avoided drilling the hole near the seam.

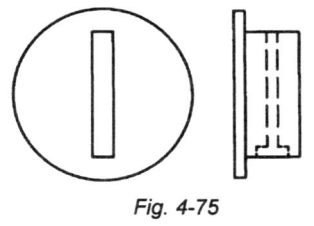

A shallow (1/64 inch deep) flange was pressed around the inside of the magazine tube at the receiver end to keep the magazine follower inside the tube during removal. The receiver end of the takedown magazine tube was also beveled slightly to make it easier to insert into the takedown extension. Be sure to reinsert the takedown magazine tube carefully to avoid damaging the beveled edge, which could cause cartridges to hang up.

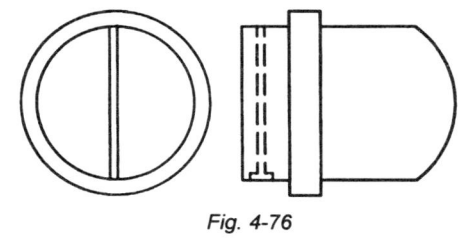

Fig. 4-75

Magazine End Plugs For Non-Takedown Rifles and Carbines

Fig. 4-76

Eight different types of magazine end plugs were used on the M1886 and are described in Table 4-15, opposite. All but Types 7 and 8 were held in place in the magazine tube by either a short or long screw. If a long screw was used, the hole was bored through the magazine end cap and one end of the hole was

Winchester Lever Action Repeaters

TABLE 4-15
M1886 MAGAZINE END PLUGS FOR NON-TAKEDOWN RIFLES AND CARBINES

Type	Face Style	Diameter (inches)	Screw Driver Slot	Screw Type	Lip	Flange Diameter	Comments—used on . . .
1	Flat	41/64	Yes	Short	Yes	None	Rifles, rarely on carbines. See Figure 4-74
2	Flat	41/64	Yes	Long	No	None	Rifles, some carbines. Like Type 1 but without lip. Screw hole bored through See Figure 4-75
3	Flat	41/64	Yes	Short	No	None	Often on carbines held by front barrel bands. Like Type 2 but with short screw
4	Round	41/64	Yes	Short	Yes	None	Rifles with fractional length magazine tubes and round barrels. Round face. See Figure 4-76

The Models of 1886 and 1892

5	Round	41/64	Yes	Long	No	None	Rifles, rarely on carbines. Like Type 4 only without lip and with screw hole bored through.
6	Round	41/64	Yes	Short	No	None	Rifles, some carbines. Like Type 5 but with short screw hole. See Figure 4-77
7	Round	41/64	No	None	No	23/32	Half Magazine or Button Magazines. See Figure 4-78.
8	Flat	41/64	No	None	No	None	Type 1 Carbine forearm only. Figure 4-79

threaded for a distance of 7/32 inches. If a short screw was used, then the hole was bored into the magazine

Fig. 4-77

end cap for only a distance for 7/32 of an inch, and threaded for its entire length.

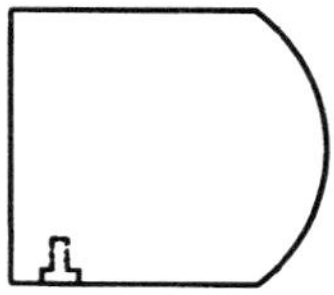

Magazine End Plug Screws

The short magazine end plug screw was 9/32 inches long overall. Its head was 13/64 inches in diameter by

Fig. 4-78

1/16 inches high. The shank was 1/8 inch in diameter and threaded 6-48 its entire length.

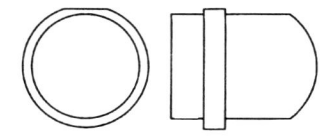

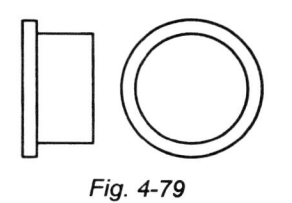

Fig. 4-79

Winchester Lever Action Repeaters

The long magazine screw was 25/32 inches long overall. Its head was 13/64 inches in diameter by 1/16 high. The shank was 1/8 inches in diameter and threaded 6-48 for 7/32 inches just below the head. The balance of the shank was unthreaded. This screw penetrated both walls of the magazine, the magazine end cap and the blind hole in the bottom of the barrel.

Magazine Followers

The magazine follower was a hollow tube open on one end for the magazine spring. The M1886 magazine follower was unique to that gun and cannot be substituted for the follower in any other model, nor can any other follower be used in the Model 1886. The same follower was used for all calibers. See Figure 4-80.

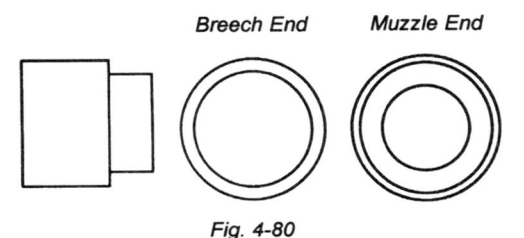

Fig. 4-80

The magazine follower was 5/8 inches in diameter at its widest point, and 57/64 inches long. The closed top that bore on the bullet and pushed it into the breech was 1/2 inches in diameter.

Magazine Spring

The M1886 magazine spring was identical to that used in the Model 1876. It was 35/64 inches in diameter and made of circular, spring steel wire. The spring had a nominal 80 coils for a 26 inch barrel rifle, 75 coils for a 24 inch barrel rifle and 70 coils for a 22 inch barrel carbine, no matter the type of forearm.

NOTE: Because the cartridge was pulled into the breech largely by the action of the carrier hook, spring tension in the M1886 was reduced considerably. Approximately one inch of spring (three to four coils) should protrude when the magazine end cap is removed.

The Models of 1886 and 1892

Takedown Magazine End Plugs

Two types of takedown magazine end plug assemblies were installed on the Model 1886 takedown rifles. Both consisted of the end cap, takedown lever, magazine lever screw, end cap screw, magazine plunger and magazine plunger spring. Both types of end plugs had a slot 9/32 inches wide into which the takedown lever was fitted. Both types were made of steel and blued.

The **Type 1** takedown magazine end cap (see Figure 4-81) was flat on the front and invariably installed on takedown rifles with full length magazine tubes to circa serial #95,000 when the lightweight and extra lightweight rifles were introduced. It was 1 23/64 inches long. The forward, or outer portion was 23/32 inches in diameter and the rear or inner portion was 41/64 inches in diameter. The outside wall of the end cap was flush with the magazine tube wall.

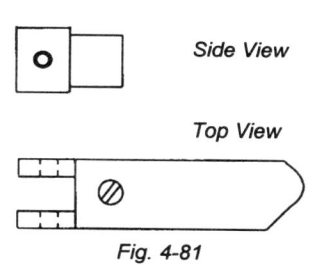

Side View

Top View

Fig. 4-81

The slot in the Type 1 end cap was 9/32 inches wide. Its end was cut on a bias; the upper portion of the slot measured 43/64 inches while the bottom slot was only 35/64 inches long. This left two side walls 7/32 inches thick.

The Type 1 magazine end cap was drilled through the walls on either side of the slot for the takedown lever screw. The hole was 9/64 inches in diameter and threaded 6-48 on the right side only. One side was counterbored 7/32 inches in diameter to accept the screw's fillister head.

The **Type 2** takedown magazine end cap was rounded on the front surface and invariably installed on lightweight, extra lightweight rifles and those takedown rifles with less than full length magazine tubes. It was 1 11/32 inches long and the forward, or outer portion was 23/32 inches in diameter. The rear or inner portion was 41/64 inches in diameter. See Figure 4-82.

Winchester Lever Action Repeaters

The slot in the Type 2 end cap was 9/32 inches wide. Its end was cut square and it was 21/32 inches deep. The walls on either side were 7/32 inches wide.

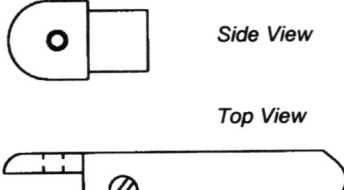

The Type 2 magazine end cap was drilled through the sidewalls for the takedown lever screw. The hole was 9/64 inches in diameter and threaded 6-48 on its right side only. One side was counterbored 7/32 inches in diameter to accept the screw's fillister head.

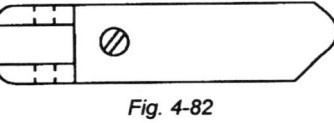

Fig. 4-82

Takedown Magazine Takedown Levers
The takedown lever used on the **Type 1** magazine end cap was shaped like the letter "L". The long stroke was 17/64 inches wide and 2 5/64 inches long. The short stroke was 29/32 inches long with a locking cam 5/32 inches wide by 1/8 inch high. There was no rebate at the end of the long stroke. See Figure 4-83.

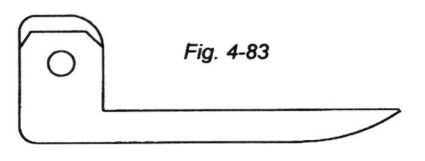

Fig. 4-83

The locking cam rotated into a groove cut on the underside of the barrel to prevent the takedown magazine tube from unscrewing until the lever was raised. The barrel groove was located on the underside of the barrel to match the length of the magazine tube.

The takedown lever used on the **Type 2** magazine end cap was also shaped like "L". The long stroke was 17/64 inches wide and 2 3/64 inches long overall. The short stroke was 13/16 inches long. It lacked a locking cam at the end of the short stroke, and the back of the long stroke where it joined the head or short stroke was rebated 1/32 inch. See Figure 4-84.

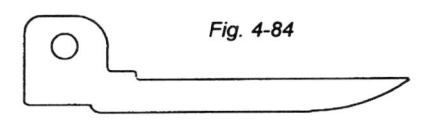

Fig. 4-84

The Models of 1886 and 1892

Both takedown levers pivoted in the magazine end cap on the magazine lever screw which was 23/32 inches long overall. It had a fillister head 13/64 inches in diameter and 3/32 inches high. The screw shank was 1/8 inch in diameter, was 5/8 inches long and threaded 6-48 for 9/32 inches of its length on the end.

Both magazine tube end caps were secured to the takedown magazine tube with the standard short magazine tube end plug screw.

Magazine Plunger and Spring

The magazine plunger was shaped from steel and case hardened. It was 7/32 inches in diameter and 3/8 inches long. The plunger spring was made of round steel wire wound into seven coils. The spring's outside diameter was 3/16 inches and it was 7/16 inches long. The spring was mounted in a hole drilled into the base of the takedown magazine end cap, at the bottom of the takedown lever slot. The plunger and plunger spring maintained pressure on the takedown lever to hold it in the closed position. See Figure 4-85.

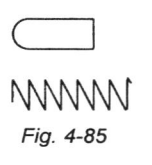

Fig. 4-85

Magazine Tube Ring

The M1886 magazine tube ring was similar to that of all other models, but had a larger interior and exterior diameter than any except for the M1876 which was even larger. See Figure 4-86. Four types of magazine tube rings were used and are listed in Table 4-16.

The **Type 1** M1886 magazine tube ring base was used on all standard barrels. It was 31/64 inches wide by 53/64 inches long by 1/16 inches high. The ring was 9/16 inches long at the base and tapered to 7/16 inches long at the outer edge. The inner diameter of the ring was 3/4 inches wide and the outer diameter was 13/16 inches. The base was drilled through with a 5/64 inch diameter hole for the magazine tube ring pin.

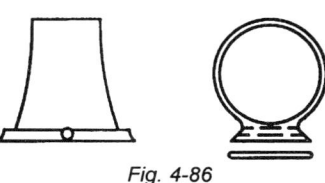

Fig. 4-86

Winchester Lever Action Repeaters

M1886 rifles with heavy or extra-heavy barrels used standard magazine tube rings which did not completely fill the elliptical slot.

TABLE 4-16 MAGAZINE TUBE RING SLOT BARREL LOCATIONS	
BARREL TYPE	DISTANCE BEHIND MUZZLE*
Standard Non-Takedown	3 13/64 ± 1/8
Heavy and Extra Heavy Non-Takedown	3 13/64 ± 1/8
Standard Barrel Takedown Rifle	2 31/32 ± 1/8
Lightweight and Extra Lightweight Takedown Rifle	2 5/8 ± 1/8
* Measurement was from muzzle to forward edge of cutout in inches	

Type 2 M1886 magazine tube rings without a magazine tube ring pin hole were used on all M1886 takedown rifles to permit the magazine tube to be removed during disassembly, and as the second ring with barrels over 30 inches long. All other dimensions remained identical to the Type 1 magazine tube ring.

The **Type 3** M1886 magazine tube ring base was narrower at 13/32 inches wide. It was used on all rapid taper barrels, round or octagon. It was drilled with a 5/64 inch diameter hole for the magazine tube ring pin. All other dimensions remained the same as the Type 1.

Type 4 M1886 magazine tube rings without a magazine tube ring pin hole were used on all lightweight, extra lightweight and special order rapid taper barrels—round or octagon—takedown rifles. All dimensions remained identical to the Type 3 magazine tube ring.

The elliptical cuts in all rapid taper barrels were quite shallow and the rings worked loose easily when withdrawing the magazine tube on takedown variations. Care must be taken not to damage the thin lips.

The Models of 1886 and 1892

Magazine Tube Ring Pin

The magazine tube ring pin for the M1886 rifle was 5/64 inches in diameter by 1/2 inch long. It was made from steel wire and blued. Refer to Figure 4-86.

Rear Sights
Rifle Rear Sights

Rifles were equipped with both the ladder-type and semi-buckhorn rear sights. The selection of the rear sight type, unless specified in a special order, appears to have been left to the individual assembler. Both types were installed with equal frequency to circa serial #110,000; after, the semi-buckhorn-type began to predominate. After circa serial #130,000, the ladder-type was rarely installed except on special order rifles that may have been assembled outside their serial range.

The M1886 ladder-type rear sight used on rifles and some carbines was longer than those used on previous models, except some Model 1876s. The base was 2 9/16 inches long and 49/64 inches wide at its widest point (both measurements are ± 1/64 inches reflecting the amount of polishing prior to bluing). The ladder was 2 9/16 inches long and was designed to be raised vertically. This sight was often, but not always, marked "1886" across the top of the ladder, below the leaf retention screw. It was usually installed on special order barrels that were shorter than standard. See Figure 4-87.

Fig. 4-87

Elevation adjustments were made by raising or lowering the "leaf" or "step" which was 3/4 inches wide by 7/32 inches high and 1/8 inches thick. The leaf had a sighting "V" notch in the center, cut 7/32 inches wide by 3/32 inches deep.

Winchester Lever Action Repeaters

The semi-buckhorn-type rifle rear sight had serrations on the sides of the "horns" to make it easier to lift the sight for elevation adjustments using the angular, stepped elevator. Figure 4-88.

The semi-buckhorn rear sight was 3 1/32 ± 1/32 inches long overall. It was 21/32 ± 1/64 inches wide at the base where it slid into the rear sight dovetail. The "buckhorns" at the rear were 31/64 ± 1/64 inches high

Fig. 4-88

The cutout in the semi-buckhorn sight for the elevator varied from 3/32 to 7/64 inches wide and 5/8 to 13/16 inches long.

NOTE: The length of the elevation slide cutout is not important, but the *width* is. Marlin firearms were equipped with semi-buckhorn rear sights similar to the Winchester design but with elevation slide cutouts 5/64 inches wide. Both Winchester and Marlin rear sight dovetails were 3/8 inches wide. Measure the elevation slide cutout carefully to distinguish between the two types.

Three types of rear sight elevators were installed on Model 1886 rifles using the semi-buckhorn rear sight.

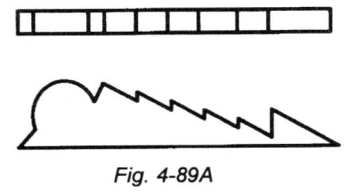

Fig. 4-89A

Type 1 elevators (see Figure 4-89A) had a straight front wall, were 7/64 inches wide by 1 3/32 inches long and had six adjustment steps in 100 yard increments for 100 to 600 yards. The Type 1 was used throughout production and almost exclusively to circa serial #75,000. It was unmarked.

After circa serial #75,000, the **Type 2** rear sight elevator (see Figure 4-89B) began to appear, although rarely. It was 3/32 inches wide by 1

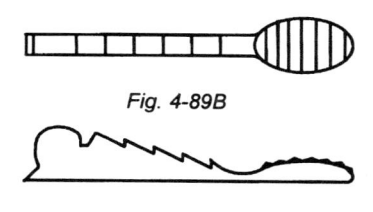

The Models of 1886 and 1892

Fig. 4-89B

21/32 inches long and had a serrated, nearly flat thumbpiece at the rear that could be pushed to increase elevation. It had six steps in 100 yard increments to 600 yards. The thumbpiece was 1/4 inch wide at its widest point, by 25/64 inches long and oval in shape when viewed from above. The thumbpiece had seven grooves or serrations milled diagonally across its entire width and was unmarked.

The **Type 3** rear sight elevator (see Figure 4-89C) was identical to the Type 2, except for patent dates roll marked on the left side in non-serif letters and numbers, reading from the muzzle end:

PAT.FEB.5.1901.

Fig. 4-89C

The patent date line was 21/32 inches long and the letters and numbers were 1/16 inches high. There were no spaces between words and/or numbers as proper punctuation would dictate. Periods were used in lieu of commas.

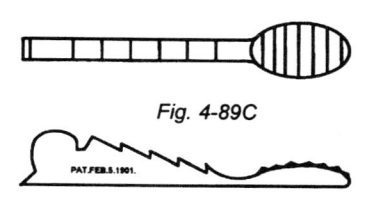

Carbine Rear Sights

The standard rear sight used on most M1886 carbines was the same ladder-type installed on all other lever action models, but with differing range gradations. The top arch of the ladder was sometimes, but not always roll-marked with the sight's year of introduction, "1873". See Figure 4-90.

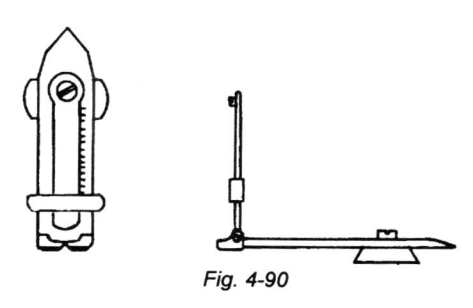

Fig. 4-90

The sight base was 11/64 ± 1/64 inches wide at the widest point by 1 29/32 ± 1/64 inches long. The ladder was 1 3/4 ± 1/64 inches long.

Winchester Lever Action Repeaters

Some carbines were fitted with the longer ladder style rear sight used on the M1886 rifle, usually on the larger caliber carbines.

The M1886 carbine was never equipped with the semi-buckhorn rear sight, except possibly on special order. A genuine example has thus far proven elusive.

Special Order Rear Sights
Special order sights for both carbines and rifles were available from Winchester, but only the tang sight and the side-mounted receiver sight seem to have been ordered with any frequency. The Winchester tang sight factory-installed on the upper tang of the M1886 was unique to this model and is rare and expensive to replace. The tang sight post was mounted much farther to the rear on the base so that the bolt can open fully without striking the post. The sight post was centered on the base, not forward as on other models and is, accordingly, much longer. See Figure 4-91.

The tang sight base was 2 11/16 inches long. The mounting screw holes were 2 3/16 inches apart, center to center. These measurements were the same on all Winchester tang sight bases. The sight post was mounted 1 7/16 to 1 1/2 inches behind the front edge of the base compared to 13/16 to 7/8 inches for all other tang sight variations.

Fig. 4-91

The side-mounted receiver sights installed by Winchester were manufactured by Lyman and Marbles. Lyman codes were as follows: for "**N1**", all .33 caliber rifles and carbines. "**N**", all other calibers. Marbles codes were: "**W4 1/2**" for .33 caliber rifles and carbines. "**W4**" for all other calibers.

The side-mounted receiver sight factory installed on the M1886—regardless of how it was coded on the inside of the shaft—must measure

The Models of 1886 and 1892

3 1/2 inches long from the center of the front mount, or pivot, screw hole, to the center of the rear, or pointer, screw hole. See Figures 4-92. Any Lyman receiver sight installed on a Model 1886 which measures 3 5/16 inches center-to-center between these two screws was not factory installed and was originally intended for use on either a M1892 or M1894 Winchester. The presence of this special order side-mounted receiver sight if factory installed, will increase the collector value of the gun modestly, while the presence of the non-factory-original M1892 or M1894 sight will greatly detract from the value of the gun.

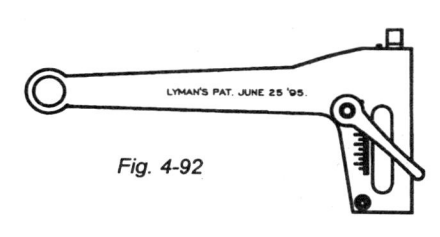

Fig. 4-92

The Model 1895 Lyman-manufactured receiver sight was coded "**WR**" or "**WT**". It's dimensions were exactly the same as the Lyman-manufactured M1886 receiver sight. If found installed on a M1886, even though coded for a Model 1895, it was probably factory installed. On rare occasions when the Lyman side-mounted rear sight was installed on a M1886, a dovetail was not milled into the top of the barrel for the standard rear sight unless the customer specifically requested it.

NOTE: The author has spent many years examining the codes stamped on the side-mounted receiver sights and has concluded that the only way to determine authenticity is to carefully measure the distance between the screw holes, then obtain a factory letter verifying its originality.

Front Sights
Rifle Front Sights
Standard front sights installed on the M1886 rifles were made of one piece of steel. Front sights with steel bases and nickel-silver blades were also used interchangeably. The all-steel blade and base were cast in one piece and machined to shape. The nickel-silver blade was press-fitted into a slot in the steel base.

Winchester Lever Action Repeaters

The M1886 front sight base was 5/8 inches wide by 11/32 inches long and was fitted into a 3/8 inch long dovetail, as on other models. The sides of the sight blade tapered slightly outward from top to bottom. See Figure 4-93.

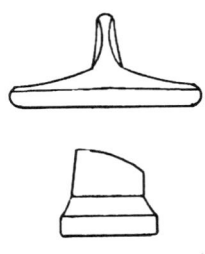

The front sight dovetail on standard, heavy and extra-heavy rifle barrels was 3/8 inches wide and located 3/4 ± 1/32 inches behind the muzzle. This distance can often be used to determine whether or not a barrel has been cut back at the muzzle end.

Fig. 4-93

Sight bases on special order lightweight and extra lightweight barrels were fitted to the curve of the barrel and silver soldered in place as the barrel was too thin to accept a dovetail cut. The front sight blade and base was then pressed into a dovetail in the front sight base. This front sight configuration became standard on the continuation Model 71.

Carbine Front Sights
Two types of front sights were installed by soldering onto the M1886 carbine barrel. Keep in mind that the front barrel band was always installed behind the front sight in this model.

The **Type 1** front sight for the M1886 carbine was the one piece steel post/blade which measured 19/64 inches wide by 11/32 inches long and 21/64 inches high. This was essentially the same front sight installed on later variations of the M1866 and M1873, after the front barrel band/front sight was discontinued. This was the predominant type of carbine front sight for the M1886 carbine. See Figure 4-94.

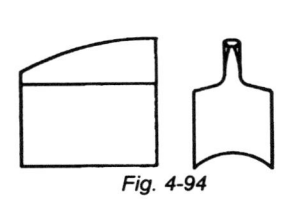

Fig. 4-94

The **Type 2** carbine front sight was installed intermittently throughout production. It was a steel post soldered to the barrel 23/32 inches

The Models of 1886 and 1892

behind the muzzle. A blade was fitted into a slot in the base and secured with steel pin that penetrated the walls of the post and the blade. The blade was made of steel, brass, nickel, silver, ivory or any combination of these materials. See Figure 4-95.

The Type 2 post was 9/32 inches wide by 7/32 inches high by 11/32 inches long. The blade was 1/16 inches wide by 11/32 inches long by 21/64 inches high. The pin was 1/16 inches in diameter by 19/64 inches long which meant that the pin ends protruded slightly. This was normal and does not necessarily indicate a replacement pin.

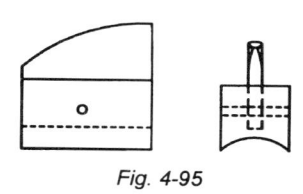

Fig. 4-95

On special order, M1886 carbines were fitted with a rifle front sight which was installed in a dovetail near the muzzle. In this case, the width of the front sight base was always reduced to permit the installation of the front barrel band.

NOTE: The front barrel band on the M1886 carbine has to be turned upside down to slip over the barrel and front sight, then tilted back and rotated until the magazine tube can be inserted through the lower opening. The barrel band screw enters from the left.

M1886 Screw Types and Sizes

Screws for the M1886 that were common to more than one model Winchester are shown in Table 4-17. The thread sizes for all M1886 screws are shown in Table 4-18.

Winchester Lever Action Repeaters

TABLE 4-17 MODEL 1886 SCREWS COMMON TO MORE THAN ONE MODEL	
Buttplate screw	1866, 1873, 1876, 1892, 1894, 1895
Forearm tip screw	1866, 1873, 1876, 1892, 1894
Magazine end plug screw, short	1866, 1873, 1876, 1892, 1894
Rear sight lock screw, ladder sight	1866, 1873, 1876, 1892, 1894
Ladder rear sight leaf or step retaining screw	1866, 1873, 1876, 1892, 1894
Sear and trigger spring screw	1866, 1892
Tang screw (stock bolt)	1876
Tang screw, lower	1866 (late), 1873, 1876
Tang sight mount hole plug screw	1866, 1873, 1876, 1892, 1894
Trigger spring screw	1866, 1892

The Models of 1886 and 1892

TABLE 4-18 MODEL 1886 SCREW THREAD SIZES	
SCREW	THREAD
Cartridge guide screw	6-48
Cartridge stop screw	3/16-36
Carrier spring screw	5/32-32
Forearm tip screw	6-48
Front band screw, carbine	4-56
Hammer screw	1/4-30
Magazine lever screw, takedown	6-48
Magazine end plug screw, long	6-48
Magazine end plug screw, short	6-48
Mainspring strain screw	9-32
Rear band screw, carbine	4-56
Sear and trigger spring screw	6-48
Saddle ring stud	1/4-30
Spring cover screw	3/16-36
Tang sight mount hole plug screw	3/16-36
Tang screw (stock bolt)	12-28
Trigger spring screw	6-48

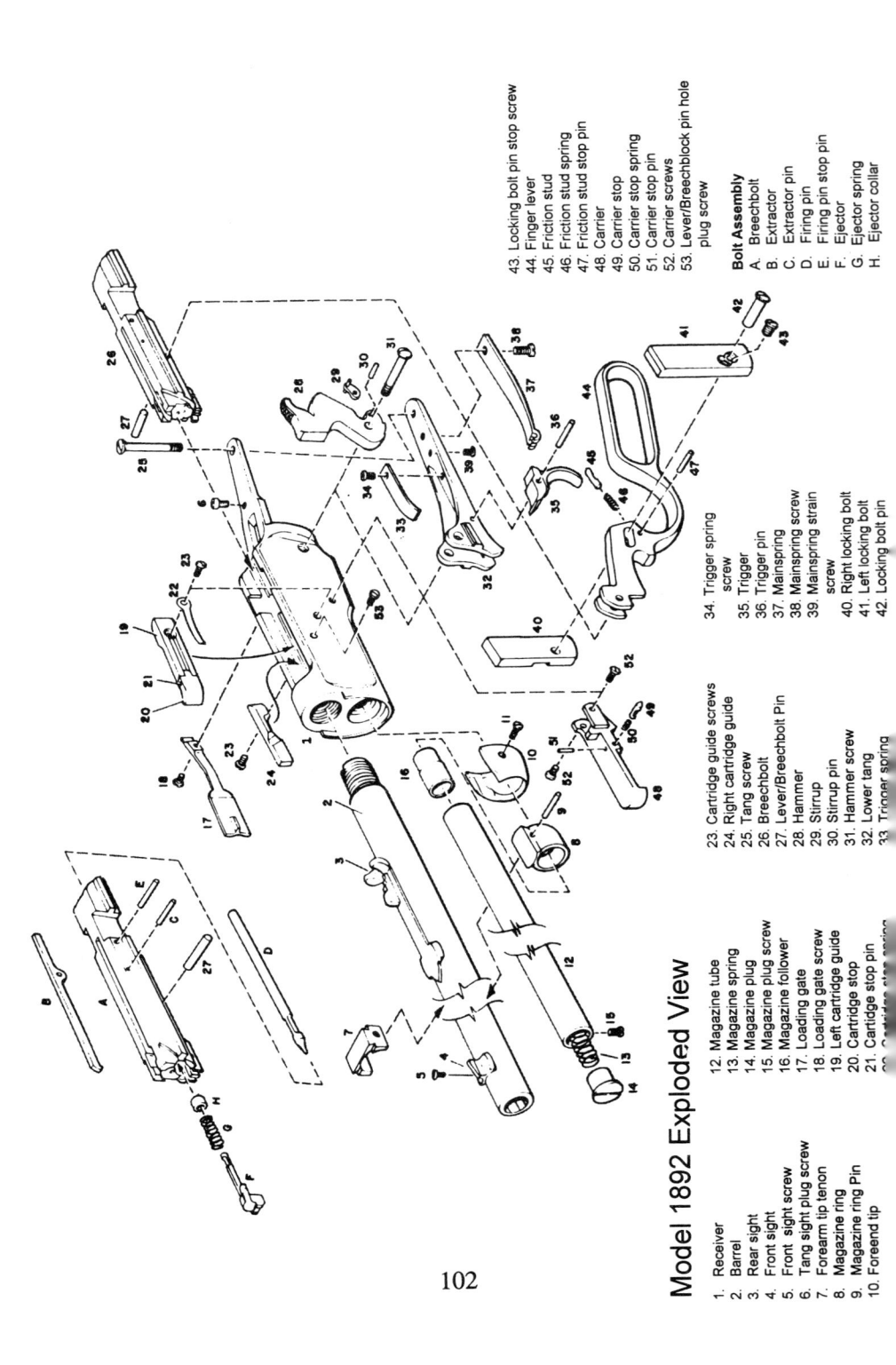

Model 1892 Exploded View

1. Receiver
2. Barrel
3. Rear sight
4. Front sight
5. Tang sight plug screw
6. Forearm tip tenon
7. Magazine ring
8. Magazine ring Pin
9. Foreend tip
10.
12. Magazine tube
13. Magazine spring
14. Magazine plug
15. Magazine plug screw
16. Magazine follower
17. Loading gate
18. Loading gate screw
19. Left cartridge guide
20. Cartridge stop
21. Cartridge stop pin
23. Cartridge guide screws
24. Right cartridge guide
25. Tang screw
26. Breechbolt
27. Lever/Breechbolt Pin
28. Hammer
29. Stirrup
30. Stirrup pin
31. Hammer screw
32. Lower tang
33. Trigger spring
34. Trigger spring screw
35. Trigger
36. Trigger pin
37. Mainspring
38. Mainspring screw
39. Mainspring strain screw
40. Right locking bolt
41. Left locking bolt
42. Locking bolt pin
43. Locking bolt pin stop screw
44. Finger lever
45. Friction stud
46. Friction stud spring
47. Friction stud stop pin
48. Carrier
49. Carrier stop
50. Carrier stop spring
51. Carrier stop pin
52. Carrier screws
53. Lever/Breechblock pin hole plug screw

Bolt Assembly
A. Breechbolt
B. Extractor
C. Extractor pin
D. Firing pin
E. Firing pin stop pin
F. Ejector
G. Ejector spring
H. Ejector collar

The Models of 1886 and 1892

CHAPTER 5 THE MODEL OF 1892

The Winchester Model 1892 is essentially a scaled-down Model 1886, designed to fire the shorter cartridges which, although originally developed for the Model 1873, had remained immensely popular nineteen years later. The Model 1892 was intended to replace the Model 1873 whose reputation for reliability and effectiveness lived on in the hearts and minds of Americans long after shipments ended in 1923.

Designed by the quintessential firearms genius, John Moses Browning, the Model 1892 is perhaps the most popular with collectors of all the lever action Winchesters. A plentiful supply and reasonable costs have, over the years kept this particular model alive in the imaginations, and cherished in the hearts, of antique firearms collectors the world over.

The M1892 was manufactured as shown in Table 5-1

TABLE 5-1 MODEL 1892 WINCHESTER VARIATIONS*		
VARIATION	NUMBER	% OF PRODUCTION
Rifle	667,000	65%
Carbine	334,000	33%
Musket	Unknown	Less than 2%
TRIGGERS		
TYPE	NUMBER	% OF PRODUCTION
Plain	995,000	99%
Set	6,000	1%
MAGAZINES		
TYPE	NUMBER	% OF PRODUCTION
Full	999,000	99%

Winchester Lever Action Repeaters

Half	1,214	Less than 1%
2/3	403	Less than 1%
3/4	52	Less than 1%

STOCKS		
VARIATION	**NUMBER**	**% OF PRODUCTION**
Straight grip	999,603	99%
Pistol grip	1,721	Less than 1%
Checkered	1,252	Less than 1%

BARRELS		
VARIATION	**NUMBER**	**% OF PRODUCTION**
Round	333,775	33%
Octagon	660,874	66%
Half round/half octagon	6,675	Less than 1%

BARREL LENGTH (INCHES)		
LENGTH	**NUMBER**	**% OF PRODUCTION**
24 inches	665,000	66%
26 inches	Approximately 800	Less than 1%
20 inches	333,000	33%
14-19 inches (carbine)	Approximately 1,200	Less than 1%
21-23 inches (rifle)	Approximately 800	Less than 1%

The Models of 1886 and 1892

27-36 inches (rifle)	Approximately 35	Less than 1%
CALIBERS		
CALIBER	NUMBER	% OF PRODUCTION
218 Bee (1938)	Approximately 1,300	Less than 1%
.25-20 W.C.F. (1895)**	40,000	4%
.32-20 W.C.F. (1895)	75,000	7%
.38-40 W.C.F. (1879)	85,000	8%
.44-40 W.C.F. (1873)	800,000	80%

* The numbers shown in this table are estimates based on the Author's research in factory records at the Cody Firearms Museum, Buffalo Bill Historical Center, Cody, WY
** Although the .25-20 was considered a standard caliber after circa serial #800,000, it did not prove very popular, which accounts for its low rate of production.

Factory records for the M1892, as with all other Winchester firearms prior to 1923, are held at the Cody Firearms Museum, Buffalo Bill Historical Center, Cody Wyoming. On request, the Museum will provide a letter with all recorded information regarding a specific serial number. M1892 records for serial numbers 1 through 379,999 are on file. See Appendix H.

Buttplates

The M1892, until the very last months of production, used only two styles of buttplates, one each on standard rifles and carbines, but with type variations. Rifle buttplates were crescent in shape and had a short upper tang. A modified shotgun-type buttplate was installed on the majority of M1892 carbines. On special order, approximately 1,500 M92s were fitted with non-standard buttplates: 1,350 were fitted with hard rubber buttplates, 150 were fitted with Swiss-style buttplates.

Winchester Lever Action Repeaters

Buttplates—Rifle

Two types of buttplates were installed on rifles as a standard feature. The **Type 1** "rifle style" or "crescent buttplate" was installed on the vast majority of M1892 rifles. It was 4 1/8 ± 1/8 inches long from the top of the tang to the toe. It was ovoid in shape and 1 inch wide at the base of the tang. It flared to 1 19/64 inches at its widest point slightly above the center and tapered to 3/4 inches wide, 1/4 inch above the toe. These dimensions will vary by 1/16 of an inch depending on the amount of polishing the buttplate received before finishing. See Figure 5-1.

The Type 1 tang on the crescent buttplate was 1 35/64 ± 1/16 inches long from front to rearmost point and was uniformly 59/64 ± 1/32 inches wide.

The toe of the Type 1 crescent buttplate angled to the rear in a gentle curve, hence the name, "crescent buttplate" assigned by collectors.

The Type 1 crescent buttplate had two 1/4 inch diameter unthreaded holes, countersunk to 11/32 inches in diameter, for the buttplate screws. The top hole was located on the tang 7/16 inches from the front edge to the hole's center. The bottom screw hole was 1 1/4 inches above the toe. The screw holes were not reinforced on the inner surface and the shoulders of the buttplate screws were beveled to fit snugly into the countersunk holes so that the tops of the screws were flush with the outer surface. Both screw holes were centered on the buttplate's width.

Fig. 5-1

Late in M1892 production (circa serial #980,000), the **Type 2** serrated steel shotgun buttplate, identical to those on the M53 and M65, was used occasionally but almost always in conjunction with the hooded ramp front sight. See Figure 5-2.

The Models of 1886 and 1892

It was 5 ± 1/32 inches high overall by 1 27/64 inches wide at the widest point. The top screw hole was 19/32 ± 1/32 inches below the top of the buttplate and the bottom screw hole was exactly 1 ± 1/32 inches above the toe—the holes were 3 3/8 inches apart, center-to-center. The plate had 39 horizontal serrations to a depth of approximately 1/64 of an inch. In profile, the buttplate was flat on the inner surface.

NOTE: Marlin firearms were fitted with a similar buttplate but one with only 35 horizontal serrations rather than 39. The screw holes were only 2 27/32 inches apart, center-to-center and the Marlin buttplate "leaned" slightly forward at the toe. While this buttplate could be installed on a Winchester M92, it would have to be flattened and new holes would have to be drilled into the stock to accommodate the Marlin butt plate screw pattern.

Fig. 5-2

Other styles of buttplates were installed only on special order rifles with the exception of those early M1892 rifles manufactured for export to South America. Many M1873 parts, including buttplates, were used on these rifles.

Buttplates—Carbines

Three types of buttplates were standard on the M1892 Carbine.

The most common was the **Type 1** "modified shotgun-style" buttplate made of steel. It was 4 1/4 ± 1/8 inches long and ovoid in shape. The Type 1 plate was 1 1/32 ± 1/32 inches wide and flared to 1 21/64 inches ± 1/32 inches wide at its widest point approximately two-thirds of the distance from the top, narrowing to 29/32 ± 1/32 inches wide, 1/4 inch above the toe. See Figure 5-3.

Fig. 5-3

Winchester Lever Action Repeaters

The M1892 carbine buttplate tang was 1 1/32 ± 1/32 inches wide and 1 15/16 ± 1/16 inches long overall. The tang extended forward across the top of the buttstock 19/32 inches to a point where it tapered abruptly inward to 19/32 inches wide. It extended forward another 1 11/32 inches to end in a round tip.

Two unthreaded holes were drilled in the M1892 buttplate to attach it to the stock. Both were 1/4 inches in diameter and countersunk to 11/32 inches. The top screw hole was located on the tang 39/64 inches from the rounded front, the bottom hole was 1 3/32 inches above the toe. Both holes were centered on the plate's width.

The top screw hole on the M1892 carbine buttplate was not reinforced although the bottom screw hole was.

The **Type 2** shotgun-style buttplate used on either the rifle or carbine was a special order feature. It was 5 ± 1/8 inches long and ovoid in shape. The width, at the widest part was 1 9/16 ± 1/16 inches.

Four variations of the Type 2 shotgun-style buttplate were installed on the M1892 carbine by Winchester. The **Type 2A** was made of steel and had a smooth, unchecked surface. It had a tang 5/16 inches long at the top of the plate. Buttplate screw holes were located 3 inches apart, center to center. See Figure 5-4.

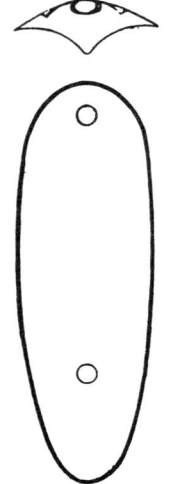

Fig. 5-4

The **Type 2B** shotgun-style buttplate was also made of steel and was checkered, with 16 diamonds to the inch. Buttplate screw holes were located 3 3/8 inches apart, center to center. The tang on the Type 2 buttplate was 5/16 inches long. They resembled those installed on the early Model 70 Rifles. See Figure 5-5.

The Models of 1886 and 1892

The **Type 2C** shotgun-style buttplate was made of hard rubber and was rarely installed on the M1892, and will command a slight premium if factory-installed. It may or may not have the tang at the top like its steel counterparts. Buttplate screw holes were located 3 3/32 inches apart, center to center. Winchester purchased hard rubber buttplates from other makers. As they cost more than the "in-house-produced" steel buttplates, they were only installed when a special order specifically requested the hard rubber buttplate.

The **Type 2D** shotgun-style buttplate was installed only on the very last production M1892s from circa serial #980,000 on. It was flat, lacked a tang, was made of steel and had 39 serrations cut 1/64 inches deep across the width between the two buttplate screw holes. The buttplate screw holes were 3 3/8 inches apart, center to center. The Type 2D buttplate was also installed on the continuation M53 and M65 and on late M94 carbines. Refer to Figure 5-2.

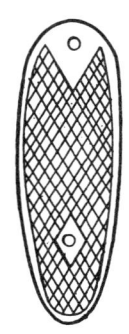

Fig. 5-5

NOTE: Extensive research into the Winchester records at the Cody Firearms Museum, Buffalo Bill Historical Center at Cody, Wyoming has shown that if the hard rubber shotgun-style buttplate was installed, the records will usually so state. But if the records list only the buttstock as "shotgun", the steel shotgun-style buttplate was invariably installed. It is the author's opinion however, that if a hard-rubber shotgun-style buttplate is found on a Model 1892 and the wood is "proud" all the way around, then the hard rubber buttplate is probably factory original, even if the factory records do not so state. The wood should be "proud" just enough to catch a fingernail. As most special order guns were subjected to extra finishing, the wood on these rare and very desirable guns will be slightly more "proud" than on standard finish stocks.

NOTE: Do not confuse Winchester and Marlin steel shotgun-style buttplates. Marlin steel buttplates had a slight forward curve to the toe and the screw holes were 2 27/32 inches apart.

Winchester Lever Action Repeaters

The **Type 3** M1892 carbine buttplate was a modification of the rifle crescent buttplate. It was installed, although rarely, on the M1892 carbine on special order. The toe of this carbine buttplate was angled forward toward the muzzle approximately 9/64 inches *ahead* of a center line drawn through the buttplate. All other dimensions remained the same.

Buttplates—Color Case-Hardened
The Winchester factory did install color case-hardened steel buttplates on a very few special order M1892s. A factory letter (See Appendix H) is the only sure way to confirm its originality.

Buttplate Screws
Two wood screws attached the buttplate to the stock. They were 1 3/16 inches long. The head was 11/32 inches in diameter by 1/8 inch high. The shank of the buttplate screw was 1 1/16 inches long by 7/32 inches in diameter at the head end. The screw tapered to a sharp point. The head was beveled at the shoulders so that they would fit snugly into the 11/32 inch countersink on the buttplate, thus presenting a flush surface.

Two types of buttplate screws were used. The **Type 1** screw was threaded for only the last 23/32 inches of its length and was used to circa serial #980,000. See Figure 5-6A.

Fig. 5-6A

The **Type 2** screws were used in late variations of the M1892 after circa serial #980,000. The Type 2 screw was identical to the Type 1 except that the entire shank of the screw was threaded. See Figure 5-6B.

NOTE: Some "experts" have asserted that Winchester made late M1892 lever actions with "Phillip's Head" buttplate screws, identical to those found on the late varia-

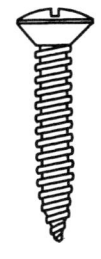

Fig. 5-6B

The Models of 1886 and 1892

tions of the M12 Shotgun. Production of the M1892 ceased in 1932 but the Phillip's head screw was only invented in the mid-1930s to permit the installation of metal aircraft coverings with power tools.

Buttstocks

With the start of M1892 production, Winchester had taken steps to tighten up its formerly lenient manufacturing tolerances to eliminate the large amount of hand work needed for stocking previous models. As a result, buttstocks are readily interchangeable between the M1892 and the later M1894 rifles and carbines. In fact, rifle buttstocks *are* interchangeable between the M1892, M1894 and M1895 *rifles*. However, the M1892/94 *carbine* stock *cannot* be interchanged with the M1895 carbine buttstock because of the shorter M1895 carbine buttplate tang.

NOTE: When determining whether or not a stock is factory-installed, check the fit and finish at all points of contact with metal parts. There should be no gaps or crevices of any kind. Note also that a stock removed from one M1894 or M1895 rifle or carbine may not fit perfectly when installed on another receiver. But the original factory-installed part will.

Buttstocks—Rifle

The rifle buttstock was 11 11/16 ± 3/32 inches from the front top at the junction of stock and receiver to the start of the buttplate tang cutout. It was 14 1/4 ± 1/8 inches long from the receiver to the toe. See Figure 5-7.

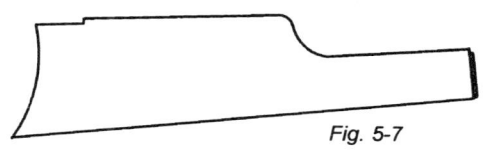

Fig. 5-7

The wrist widened from 1 5/16 ± 1/8 inches wide at the front to 1 3/8 ± 1/16 wide at the back, just below the front of the comb. From there, the stock tapered gradually to 1 11/32 ± 1/16 inches wide at the buttplate

Winchester Lever Action Repeaters

The M1892 rifle buttstock was 1 11/32 ± 1/16 inches high at the front of the wrist, 2 17/32 ± 1/16 inches high at the front of the comb and 3 9/16 ± 1/8 inches high at the rear, not including the buttplate tang cutout.

The buttplate tang cutout was 1 3/32 ± 1/32 inches long by 15/16 ± 1/64 inches wide. There was also a slight projection—an interrupted flange—approximately 3/32 inches long machined into the buttstock at the front of the wrist which mated with a corresponding milled groove on the inside of the receiver.

The stockbolt hole was drilled through the rear of the wrist. It was 7/32 inches in diameter and was not counterbored or countersunk. It was located 3 1/2 ± 1/16 inches, less the 3/32 inch flange, from the front edge of the stock and centered in the milled groove for the receiver tang.

NOTE: Only a single stock bolt attaches the M1892 rifle stock to the receiver. Winchester did not install a wood screw through the lower receiver tang as on previous models.

Two 1/4 inch diameter holes were drilled in the rear of the stock to secure the buttplate. The top hole was centered in the cutout for the buttplate tang 19/64 ± 1/32 inches behind the front of the groove. The lower hole was drilled into the rear face of the buttstock and centered 1 7/32 ± 1/16 above the toe.

Buttstocks—Carbine
Three types of carbine buttstock were installed on the M1892 carbine during its production life.

The **Type 1** carbine buttstock was 11 3/8 ± 3/16 inches long along the top, starting at the junction of stock and receiver and ending at the start of the buttplate tang cutout. The stock was 13 9/16 ± 1/8 inches long from the receiver to the toe. See Figure 5-8.

The Models of 1886 and 1892

The wrist widened from 1 5/16 ± 1/8 inches wide at the front to 1 13/32 ± 1/16 wide at the back, just below the front of the comb. From there, the stock tapered gradually to 1 11/32 ± 1/16 inches wide at the buttplate

The Type 1 carbine buttstock was 1 13/32 ± 1/16 inches high at the front of the wrist, 2 7/16 ± 3/16 inches high at the front of the comb and 4 3/16 ± 1/8 inches high at the rear, not including the buttplate tang cutout.

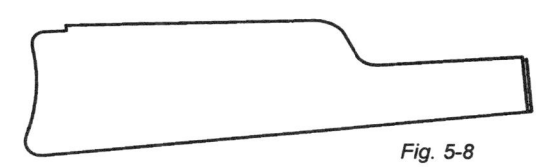

Fig. 5-8

The Type 1 carbine buttplate tang cutout was 1 7/8 inches long. It widened into three sections: 9/16 at the front, 5/8 in the middle and 1 3/64 inches wide at the rear. There was also a slight projection—an interrupted flange—approximately 3/32 inches long machined into the buttstock at the front of the wrist which mated with a corresponding milled groove on the inside of the receiver.

The stockbolt hole was drilled through the rear of the wrist. It was 7/32 inches in diameter and was not counterbored or countersunk. It was located 3 1/2 ± 1/16 inches from the front edge of the stock (less the 3/32 inch flange) and centered in the milled groove for the receiver tang.

NOTE: Only the single stock bolt holds the M1892 carbine stock to the receiver. Winchester never installed a wood screw through the lower receiver tang as on previous models.

Two 1/4 inch diameter holes were drilled in the rear of the stock to secure the buttplate. The top hole was centered in the cutout for the buttplate tang 1 19/64 ± 1/32 inches behind the front of the groove. The lower hole was drilled into the rear face of the buttstock and centered 1 5/64 ± 1/16 above the toe.

Winchester Lever Action Repeaters

The **Type 2** carbine stock was the shotgun-style. It was 12 9/16 ± 1/8 inches long from the front top at the junction of stock and receiver to the beginning of the buttplate tang cutout if the Type 1 or Type 3 carbine shotgun-style buttplate was installed, or 12 11/16 ± 1/8 inches long if the Type 2 carbine shotgun-style buttplate was used. Regardless of which shotgun-style buttplate was used, the carbine stock was 13 13/16 ± 1/8 inches long from the receiver to the toe. All other carbine stock measurements were the same as for the Type 1 carbine buttstock. See Figure 5-9.

The **Type 3** shotgun-style carbine buttstock was installed on M1892 carbines after circa serial #980,000, and on the continuation models 53, 55, 63 and 64. Those stocks were 12 11/16 ± 1/8 inches long from the front top at the junction of the stock and receiver to the rear edge and 12 7/8 ± 1/8 inches long from the receiver to the toe. Other dimensions will be the same as the Type 1 carbine buttstock.

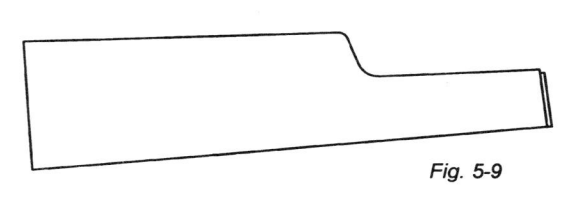

Fig. 5-9

NOTE: M1892 and M1894 buttstocks are interchangeable although some are shaped differently. For this reason you may encounter a M1892 carbine with a late M1894-type buttstock with either the Type 3 or Type 4 shotgun-style buttplate. These were factory installed very late in M1892 production, invariably with the later hooded ramp front sight. If an early M1892 carbine is found with a Type 3 or 4 shotgun-style buttplate not originally installed at the factory, then it is considered a major alteration and reduces the carbine's value accordingly.

"Eastern Carbines"

A number of M1892 carbines were manufactured with rifle-style crescent buttplates installed. These will almost always lack the saddle ring.

The Models of 1886 and 1892

Check carefully to make certain that the buttplate was installed properly and that there are no gaps or crevices between wood and metal. Also make certain that the mounting holes for the saddle ring staple have not been filled in. The Eastern Carbine, while considered rare, is generally less desirable to collectors as they lack the "romance of the west."

A carbine with a crescent buttplate *and* a saddle ring stud was a special order item and would be extremely rare today.

Gumwood Stocks

Throughout production, Winchester found it difficult and expensive to obtain enough suitable walnut to manufacture stocks, forearms and forends for the M1892. As a substitute, they often obtained supplies of "gumwood" and used it to make carbine stocks, almost exclusively. Gumwood was softer than walnut and lacked its attractive grain. They can often be identified by their dark, even surface coloring and dented appearance. Gumwood stocks lower the collector's value of a M1892 Winchester lever action carbine or rifle. It was impossible to checker or apply an extra finish to the gumwood stock, so as most special orders involved rifles, gumwood was installed almost exclusively on carbines. As gumwood was lighter, it reduced the weight of the carbine by a few ounces, as well.

Pistol Grip Stocks

M1892 rifles and carbines were furnished with pistol grip stocks on special order. Two types were used. See Table 5-2.

The **Type 1** pistol grip cap was an ebony plug used to circa serial #85,000-105,000. It was inletted into the pistol grip and finished flush around the edges. After, circa serial #85,000-105,000, the Type 1 was installed only on special order.

Winchester Lever Action Repeaters

From circa serial #85,000-105,000 to the end of production, the **Type 2** hard rubber composition grip cap was used. The hard rubber cap was finished flush with the edges of the grip but was held on by a single wood screw. See Figure 5-10.

Sling Swivels

Sling swivels were a special order item on the M1892 and were seldom ordered. Winchester installed any type of sling swivel the customer wanted when ordered, but unless the type was specified, the factory installed the "hook and eye" sling swivel.

Fig. 5-10

Rear Sling Swivel

The rear sling swivel screw with eye was 1 to 1 11/32 inches long depending on exactly which of several types were installed. The eye itself had a 3/8 inch outside diameter and a 13/64 inch inner diameter. The hole was countersunk on both sides to 19/64 inch in diameter. The shank was 7/32 inches in diameter beneath the eye. It was threaded for all of its length but the top 7/64 inches. A flange 21/64 inches in diameter and 1/32 inches high separated the eye from the shank. The hole for the sling hook was offset toward the top. See Figure 5-11.

The rear sling screw with eye was usually screwed into the lower edge of the buttstock about 4 inches forward of the toe, so that the flange rested on the wood's surface.

Front sling swivels are described on page 169.

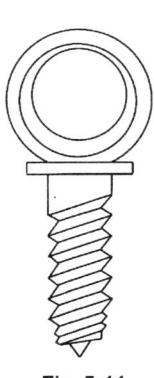

Fig. 5-11

116

The Models of 1886 and 1892

TABLE 5-2
M1892 PISTOL GRIP STOCK DIMENSIONS
(INCHES)

BUTTPLATE TYPE	POSITION	MEASUREMENTS
Crescent Buttplate		
Width of Lower Tang Cutout	Front	19/32 ± 1/32
	Rear	1/2 ± 1/32
Width of Upper Tang Cutout	Front	7/8 ± 1/32
	Rear	1/2 ± 1/32
Length of Upper Tang Cutout		3 15/16 ± 3/64, less 3/32 Flange
Length of Lower Tang Cutout Around Curve		3 7/8 ± 3/64
Length of Lower Tang Cutout, Straight		3 13/16 ± 3/64
Width of Pistol Grip Above Cap or Insert		1 1/4 ± 1/32
Height at Rear, Less Buttplate Tang Cutout		3 9/16 ± 1/8
Shotgun Buttplate		
Length to Front of Buttplate Toe Cutout	Less Flange	12 9/16 ± 3/32
	Plate Without Toe	12 3/4 ± 3/32
Length Front to Toe, Less Flange		13 13/16 ± 3/32
Height at Rear		5 1/32 ± 1/8
All other buttplate measurements were the same as for the non-pistol grip stock.		

Winchester Lever Action Repeaters

RECEIVERS

The M1892 receiver is shorter in length than all previous lever action receivers. Production calibers were the .218 Bee, .25-20, .32-20, .38-40 and .44-40, all relatively short cartridges. Like its predecessor, the M1886, the M1892 receiver lacked an opening in the bottom. With its double-side locking bolts, the M1892 was a strong action and, unlike the toggle-link actions of the past, could be safely fired with modern smokeless ammunition provided pressures and velocities of the original designs were not exceeded and the rifle or carbine was in good mechanical condition.

Only two types of M1892 receivers were manufactured, the standard solid receiver and the takedown receiver. See Figure 5-12.

The collector should be aware that M1892 receivers and barrels can be swapped to change calibers, within limits. The .25-20 and .32-20 receivers are interchangeable as are the .38-40 and .44-40 receivers but the .25-20/.32-20 and .38-40/.44-40 receivers are not as the entry port for the cartridges from the magazines are of different sizes. Bolts (bolt faces), ejectors, extractors, cartridge guides, cartridge stop, carrier and loading gate assemblies were compatible between .25 and .32 caliber receivers, and between .38 and .44 caliber receivers, but .25/.32 caliber parts are not interchangeable with .38/.44 caliber parts and vice-versa.

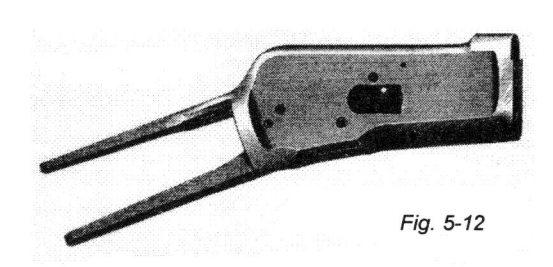

Fig. 5-12

All M1892 receivers were blued steel except in rare special order cases where color case-hardened receivers were requested. As takedown

The Models of 1886 and 1892

rifles were provided only on special order, proportionately more takedown receivers were made with color case-hardened finishes and they will command a premium. In very rare instances, "fancy finishes" were special ordered—gold, silver or nickel plating, or even "rust-browning." In many cases, a factory letter will be the only way to authenticate a special order finish. See Appendix H.

The M1892 receiver had five screw holes on the right side of the receiver and four on the left. Table 5-3 describes each.

The interior of the receiver had grooves cut into either wall. Rails on the lower tang slid into these grooves to assure the alignment between the lower tang and the action. The grooves were located at the bottom rear inside the receiver. The grooves were 53/64 inches long, 5/64 inches deep and 11/64 inches high.

The loading port cutout was rounded at the rear and slightly oval in shape at the front. It was 1 1/64 ± 1/32 inches long by 17/64 ± 1/64 inches high.

NOTE: M1892 color case-hardened receivers lost their bright colors easily compared to the color case-hardened M1873 and M1876 receivers. Winchester used a new steel for the M1892 receiver with nickel and chromium added as alloying agents. The high heat required for the case-hardening process caused chromium and nickel molecules to migrate to just below the surface. As the case colors faded, the receiver turned a silvery color that appeared similar to nickel plating.

Serial Numbers

Serial numbers to circa serial #150,000 were in san serif numbers, 5/32 inches high. Between circa serial #150,000 and 750,000, they were in san serif numbers 9/64 inches high. After circa serial # 750,000 to the end of production, they were once again in san serif numbers, 5/32 inches high.

Winchester Lever Action Repeaters

| \multicolumn{8}{c|}{TABLE 5-3 M1892 RECEIVER SCREW HOLES (INCHES)} |

No.	Name	Diameter	Counterbore Diameter	Counterbore Depth	Thread
Right					
1	Hammer Screw Hole	3/16			3/16-36
2	Loading Gate Screw Hole	1/8	3/16		None
3	Carrier Screw Hole*	3/16	7/32	1/16	3/16-36
4	Cartridge Guide Screw Hole* (Screw threaded into cartridge guide)	9/64	13/64	3/32	None
5	Finger Lever Pin Hole* (Pin Removal Only)	1/8			None
Left					
1	Hammer Screw (head) Hole*	3/16	19/64	1/8	None
2	Carrier Screw Hole*	3/16	7/32	1/16	3/16-36
3	Cartridge Guide Screw Hole*	9/64	13/64	3/32	None
4	Finger Lever Pin Stop Screw Hole*	13/64	7/32	3/64	11-36

* Hole is bored through.
NOTE: All screw heads were flush with receiver's outer surface when properly installed

The Models of 1886 and 1892

Serial number ranges for the M1892 will be found in Appendix A.

Dimensions

The dimensions for the M1892 standard and takedown receiver are shown in Table 5-4.

TABLE 5-4 M1892 RECEIVER DIMENSIONS			
		STANDARD	TAKEDOWN
Length		5 ± 1/16*	4 15/16 ± 1/16
	Loading Port to Face	1 15/16	1 7/8
Width			
	Front	1 9/32 ± 1/64	1 9/32 ± 1/64
	Center	1 3/32 ± 1/64	1 3/32 ± 1/64
	Rear	1 9/32 ± 1/64	1 9/32 ± 1/64
Height			
	Front	1 31/32	1 31/32
	Rear	2 5/32 ± 1/32	2 5/32 ± 1/32
* Tolerance variations are the result of polishing before the finish was applied. Special order variations may exhibit even more variation due to the additional polishing they would have received.			

Takedown Extension

The barrel screwed into the takedown extension which also served as a receptacle for the magazine tube. It was 1 17/64 ± 1/64 inches wide by 15/16 ± 1/64 inches long by 1 61/64 ± 1/32 inches high. The length at the top of the cutout for the barrel was 25/64 inches with no apparent deviation. See Figure 5-13.

Winchester Lever Action Repeaters

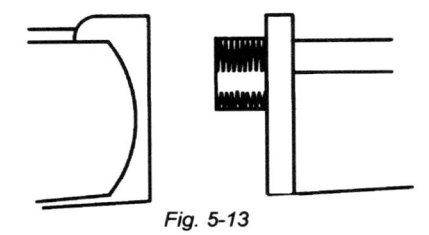

Fig. 5-13

The magazine tube guide which extended into the forearm for 17/32 inches, protruded beyond the front face of the extension 7/16 inches. It had an outer diameter of 5/8 inches and an inner diameter of 1/2 inches for the .25-20 and .32-20 caliber rifles. The outer diameter was 47/64 inches and the inner diameter was 19/32 inches for the .38-40 and .44-40 caliber rifles.

Two types of takedown extensions were used. In the **Type 1** used for the .25/.32 caliber takedown rifles, the magazine tube guide formed a complete tube. In the **Type 2** used for the .38-40 and .44-40 takedown rifles, the top arc of the magazine tube guide was cut away. See Figure 5-14.

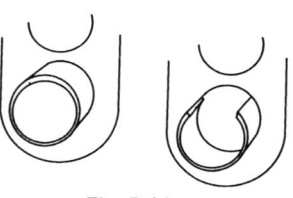

Fig. 5-14

The takedown extension housed three headless screws used to adjust the union between extension and receiver proper. The screws were 23/64 inches long overall. They had a threaded portion 3/16 inches in diameter and an unthreaded projection 9/64 inches in diameter which was 5/64 inches long. The three screws were tightened down to cause a small bulge in the rear face of the takedown extension to adjust the union between the two parts. See Figure 5-15.

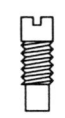

Fig. 5-15

NOTE: For a more convenient—and safer way—to adjust the union between takedown extension and receiver, start by removing the three adjusting screws. Place a flat-faced drift or punch in the screw holes and tap lightly with a small hammer to create a small bulge. Remember, the face of the takedown extension is quite thin and a pointed punch or a sharp blow could punch through. Test for the desired tightness by fitting the extension and receiver together. If you created too

The Models of 1886 and 1892

large a bulge, simply tap lightly with the hammer to reduce to the proper size. Return the screws to their screw holes to maintain the bulge and reassemble.

Upper Tang

The upper tang was machined as an integral part of the upper receiver, carried the model designation and patent dates and had two holes, one threaded and the other unthreaded. See Figure 5-16.

The front hole was used for mounting a tang sight. The front screw supplied with the tang sight passed through the tang sight base and screwed into the hole in the tang. The rear stock bolt screw was used to hold the rear of the tang sight base in place. The rear tang sight screw had a smaller head to fit down into the countersunk hole in the rear sight base.

Fig. 5-16

The front hole in the upper tang was 3/16 inches in diameter and threaded 3/16-36. It was plugged with a headless screw 3/16 inches in diameter and 9/64 inches long with a 3/16-36 thread when the tang sight was not mounted.

The rear hole was 17/64 inches in diameter and countersunk to 11/32 inches in diameter to accommodate the stock bolt screw head.

NOTE: There should be no other holes in the upper tang unless they were drilled on special order at the factory. As with all other Winchester lever actions, under no circumstances will any factory-drilled hole deface the factory-applied markings.

Winchester Lever Action Repeaters

Upper Tang Markings
The upper tang of the M1892 carried the Model designation and patent dates in seven variations.

Type 1 markings were used from the start of production to circa serial # 280,000. They included John Browning's original patent dates for the M1886, which is generally regarded as the predecessor to the M1892.

MODEL 1892.
—WINCHESTER—
PAT. OCT. 14. 1884

The top line was 1 1/16 inches long. The "M" and the numbers were 1/8 inches high, the other letters 3/32 inches high. Note the period after the date, "1892". The letters in this line *had* serifs.

The middle line was 1 5/8 inches long, including the dashes. The serifs on the letters "**W**" and "**R**" overlap the dashes slightly. These letters also often appear to be more deeply impressed than the others. The dashes were 1/4 inches long and the letters were 5/32 inches high. The letters in this line *had* serifs.

The lower line was exactly 1 inch long and the letters and numbers were 3/32 inches high. The letters in this line *lacked* serifs. The mark following the date, "**14**" appears to be a period, rather than a comma on all receivers examined. There was no period after "**1884**".

Type 2 markings were in use from circa serial #280,000-500,000.

MODEL 1892
—WINCHESTER—
TRADE MARK

The top line was 1 1/4 inches long. The letters and numbers were 7/64 inches high. The letters in this line *had* serifs. Note also that there was no period after the date, "**1892**".

The Models of 1886 and 1892

The middle line was 1 3/4 inches long, including the dashes. The letters are 9/64 inches high and again, the serifs on the "W" and "R" overlap the dashes slightly. The dashes were 1/4 inches long. The letters in this line *had* serifs.

The lower line was 7/8 inches long and the letters and numbers were 5/64 inches high. The letters in this line *lacked* serifs.

Type 3 markings were in use from circa serial #500,000-750,000. The more extensive patent information was an effort by Winchester to scare off patent infringement copies, such as the Spanish-manufactured "El Tigre."

MODEL 1892
—WINCHESTER—
TRADE MARK REG. IN U.S. PAT. OFF.

The top line was 1 7/16 inches long. The letters and numbers were 1/8 inches high. The letters in this line *had* serifs. Note also there is no period after the date, "**1892**".

The middle line was 1 13/16 inches long, including the dashes. The letters are 9/64 inches high and again, the serifs on the "W" and "R" overlap the dashes slightly. The dashes were 1/4 inches long. The letters in this line *had* serifs.

The lower line, which the author refers to as the "scare" line, was 1 23/32 inches long and the letters and numbers were 5/64 inches high. The letters in this line *lacked* serifs.

Type 4 markings were used from circa serial #750,000 to 900,000. It included additional patent office information in an attempt to scare foreign patent infringers into leaving the Winchester name off their poorly-made copies of the M1892. It read:

MODEL 1892
—WINCHESTER—
TRADE MARK REG. IN U.S. PAT. OFF. & FGN.

The top line was 1 7/32 inches long. The letters and numbers were 1/8 inches high. The letters in this line *had* serifs.

Winchester Lever Action Repeaters

The middle line was 1 13/16 inches long, including the dashes. The letters were 9/64 inches high and again, the serifs on the "W" and "R" overlap the dashes slightly. The dashes were 1/4 inches long. The letters in this line *had* serifs.

The lower line was 1 11/16 inches long and the letters and numbers were 3/32 inches high. The letters in this line *lacked* serifs.

Type 5 markings were in use from circa serial #900,000 to the end of production to eliminate reference to the M1892's 19th century origins. They read:

MODEL 92
—WINCHESTER—
TRADE MARK REG. IN U.S. PAT. OFF. & FGN.

The top line was 1 7/32 inches long. The letters and numbers were 7/64 inches high. The letters in this line *had* serifs. Note also that the numbers "**1** and **8**" were omitted from the year, 1892.

The middle line was 1 51/64 inches long, including the dashes. The letters were 1/8 inches high and again, the serifs on the "W" and "R" overlap the dashes slightly. The dashes were 1/4 inches long. The letters in this line *had* serifs.

The lower line was 1 11/16 inches long and the letters and numbers were 3/32 inches high. The letters in this line *lacked* serifs.

Type 6 upper tang markings were occasionally used on the M1892 in the very high serial number ranges circa serial #950,000 and after. It was the standard marking on the Models 53 and 65. It read:

WINCHESTER
——TRADE MARK——
-MADE IN U.S.A.-

The three lines were each 1 11/32 inches long, including dashes. The

The Models of 1886 and 1892

top line was the Winchester stylized italic logotype. The letters were 9/64 inches high and *had* serifs. The letters in the middle line were 3/64 inches high and *did not have* serifs. The letters in the bottom line were 5/64 inches high and *had* serifs.

The **Type 7** upper tang markings were only used on rifles and carbines intended for export to Great Britain or her colonies at circa serial #500,000. British import regulations at the time required that the year of introduction be stamped on the firearm. Rifles and carbines with the Type 7 address marking will have this style of Model number marking only if they were intended for export to Great Britain and her colonies. The model year was stamped behind the hammer slot, but occasionally will be found stamped elsewhere on the gun, usually on the barrel. If the rifle or carbine had the Type 7 Winchester marking but not the Model Year behind the hammer slot or on the barrel, then the rifle or carbine probably had been rejected by British customs authorities and was resold in the United States, or elsewhere.

The markings were stamped the length of the tang as usual and read:
REG. IN U.S. PAT. OFF.
—WINCHESTER—
—TRADE MARK—
The top line was 1 23/64 inches long. The letters were 5/64 inches high and *did not have* serifs.

The middle line was 1 5/8 inches long. The letters were 1/8 inches high and *had* serifs.

The bottom line was 1 45/64 inches long. The letters were 3/32 inches high and *did not have* serifs.

Finally, the model number was stamped crosswise and was centered between the rear edge of the hammer slot and the front edge of the front tang sight mount hole. It read:

Winchester Lever Action Repeaters

MOD. 1892

Both lines were 9/32 inches long and the san serif letters and numbers were 5/64 inches high

NOTE: As a general rule, the differing styles and types of upper tang markings make no difference in the collectable value of a specific rifle or carbine, providing all else is correct, and this includes the rarely encountered Type 7 upper tang marking.

Other Upper Tang Markings

If a M1892 rifle or carbine was refinished at the Winchester factory, it was often, but not always, marked either **"ORD. NO. XXX,"** or **"REFINISHED"**, or both on the left hand side of the upper tang.

Lower Tang

The lower tang of the M1892 was not an integral part of the receiver. It could be removed by removing the hammer screw and drifting the lower tang to the rear and out. The lower tang was unmarked in the M1892. There were two types of lower tangs.

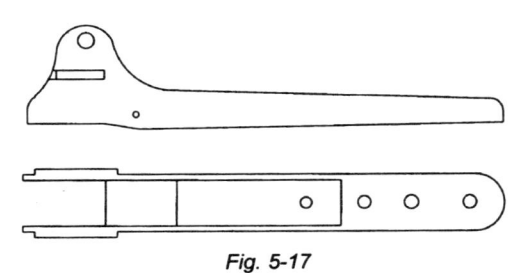

Fig. 5-17

Type 1 was the standard, straight grip tang. It was 9/16 inches wide by 4 13/16 inches long with four holes. See Figure 5-17.

Type 2 was the pistol grip lower tang. It was 9/16 inches wide by 4 3/4 long when measured straight across from one end to the other. See Figure 5-18.

Working from front to back, the first hole was for the trigger spring screw and was located 2 11/64 inches from the rear of the lower tang. It was 3/16 inches in diameter and was threaded 3/16-36.

The Models of 1886 and 1892

The second hole was for the mainspring tension screw, also called by Winchester, the "mainspring strain screw." It was located 1 3/8 inches from the rear of the lower tang and was 11/64 inches in diameter and threaded 9-32. The hole was counterbored 13/64 inches in diameter and 7/64 inches deep. The mainspring tension screw was 11/64 inches in diameter, 17/64

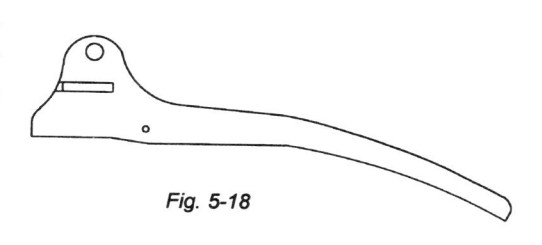

Fig. 5-18

inches long and had a 9-32 thread. Its head was 1/32 inches larger than the shank (13/64 inches in diameter). It entered from the outside and bore on the underside of the mainspring to adjust the hammer's striking force. It was not unusual for this screw to be slightly below the outer surface of the lower tang.

The third hole held the mainspring screw which penetrated the tang from the outside. It was 61/64 inches from the rear of the lower tang, 3/16 inches in diameter and unthreaded. Its counterbore was 1/4 inches in diameter and 5/32 inches deep. The mainspring screw had a slightly domed, unbeveled head 1/4 inches in diameter and 9/64 inches high. The shank was 11/64 inches in diameter, 15/64 inches long and threaded 9-32 for 11/64 inches of its length. It entered from the outside and threaded into the mainspring.

The fourth and rearmost hole was for the stock bolt, also called by Winchester, the "upper tang screw." It was located 7/16 inches from the rear edge of the tang. The hole was 13/64 inches in diameter and neither counterbored nor countersunk. It was threaded 12-28.

The lower tang interior had a rectangular slot 13/32 inches wide by 11/16 inches long milled for the trigger. The slot began 3 17/32 inches forward of the rear of the lower tang.

Winchester Lever Action Repeaters

A second cutout was milled at the front edge of the lower tang. It was 3/8 inches wide by 5/32 inches deep and formed the rear edge of the finger lever hole in the receiver.

Two holes were drilled in the sides of the lower tang. The first was for the hammer screw. It was 13/64 inches in diameter. It was unthreaded and was located 15/32 inches behind the front edge of the lower tang.

The hammer screw had a slightly domed, unbeveled head, 9/32 inches in diameter and 1/8 inches high. The shank was 3/16 inches in diameter and 1 inch long. It was threaded 3/16-36 for only 19/64 inches at the end. The hammer screw was installed through the left side of the receiver, passed through the holes in the lower tang and threaded into the right side of the receiver. The hammer screw provided a pivot for the hammer and secured the lower tang to the receiver. Both the head on the left, and the tip of the shank on the right, were flush with the receiver surface when properly installed.

The second hole was for the trigger pin. It was not threaded and was 31/32 inches behind the front edge of the lower tang. The hole was 1/8 inch in diameter.

The M1892 lower tang had two machined rails, one on either side, that fitted into corresponding grooves in the inner walls of the receiver to assure proper alignment of the lower tang with the action. The rails were 23/32 inches long and 9/64 inches high and protruded from the sides of the tang 1/16 inches.

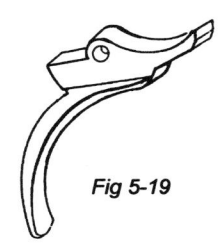

Trigger/Sear

The M1892 used a one-piece trigger and sear mechanism which was identical to and interchangeable with the M1886. It was held in the receiver by the trigger pin. See Figure 5-19.

Fig 5-19

The Models of 1886 and 1892

The trigger/sear was 3/8 inches wide at its widest point and 1 3/4 inches long overall. The sear portion was 3/8 inches wide by 1 inch long and the trigger itself was 9/32 inches wide at the top with a slight taper to 17/64 inches wide at the tip and 31/32 inches long.

The trigger/sear had a 9/64 inch diameter unthreaded hole drilled through for the trigger pin.

The trigger spring is described in the Springs section on page 152.

Trigger Pin

The trigger pin was made of hardened steel 1/8 inches in diameter and 19/32 inches long. It was press-fitted into the lower tang to serve as a pivot for the trigger. The ends of the pin were flush with the sides of the lower tang and it was held in place by the walls of the receiver. See Figure 5-20.

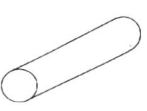

Fig. 5-20

Hammer

The M1892 hammer was 2 25/64 inches high when measured from the safety, or half-cock notch, to the uppermost tip of the spur. It was 23/64 inches wide by 1 1/2 inches from front to rear at its longest point. See Figure 5-21A.

Fig. 5-21A

Five types of hammer knurling were used on the M1892 hammer. **Type 1** was used to circa serial #200,000. It was finely checkered with 13 diamonds in 13 lines and extended across the width of the spur. It was surrounded by a decorative border (very narrow on the sides) with a small point at the top. The bottom of the border curved upward to form a slight arch. This same style of knurling was also used on early issues of the M1894. The knurled area was 5/16 inches wide

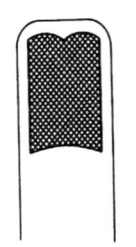

Winchester Lever Action Repeaters

by 3/8 inches high at their longest and widest points. See Figure 5-21B.

Fig. 5-21B

Type 2 was used from circa serial #200,000-350,000. It had relatively coarse checkering with 12 diamonds in 12 lines and extended across the width of the spur. It was surrounded with a plain border (quite narrow on the sides) The bottom of the border curved upward to form a slight arch. The knurled area was 5/16 inches wide by 3/8 inches high. See Figure 5-21C.

Fig. 5-21C

Fig. 5-21D

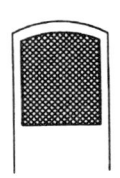

Type 3 knurling was used from circa serial #350,000-450,000. It was finely checkered with 13 diamonds in 13 lines and did not extend across the width of the hammer spur. The border was wider at the sides and ended in a straight line at the bottom of the knurling. The knurled area was 17/64 inches wide by 3/8 inches high. See Figure 5-21D.

Fig. 5-21E

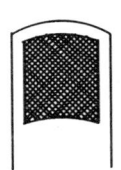

Type 4 knurling was used from circa serial #450,000-900,000. It was finely checkered with 13 diamonds in 13 lines and did not extend across the width of the hammer spur. The border was wide at the sides and ended in a slight curve at the bottom. The knurled area was 17/64 inches wide by 3/8 inches high. See Figure 5-21E.

Type 5 knurling was nearly identical to the Type 4 knurling. It was used from circa serial #900,000 to the end of production. It was finely checkered with 13 diamonds in 13 lines. The border was wide at the sides and ended in a slight curve. The collector should note that Type 5 knurling can be distinguished from the Type 4 by the fact that it was often impressed lightly and off-center so that it flared slightly from top to bottom, or else tapered so that the knurling was wider at the top than the bottom, or vice-versa. The knurled area was 9/32 inches wide by 3/8 inches high.

The Models of 1886 and 1892

NOTE: The five hammer styles can be found well outside the serial number ranges given, particularly with special order M1892s. Winchester often refilled assembler's bins before they were completely emptied of the previous run of parts. Also, when a knurling tool was worn beyond use, the toolmaker often cut the new tool with whatever pattern he wished. The type of hammer knurling will rarely increase or decrease the value of a M1892 rifle or carbine.

Hammer Screw

The hammer screw had a slightly domed, unbeveled head, 9/32 inches in diameter and 1/8 inches high. The shank was 3/16 inches in diameter and 1.0 inches long. It was threaded 3/16-36 for only 19/64 inches at the end. The hammer screw was installed through the left side of the receiver, passed through the holes in the lower tang and threaded into the right side of the receiver. The hammer screw provided a pivot for the hammer and secured the lower tang to the receiver. Both the head on the left, and the tip of the shank on the right, were flush with the receiver surface when properly installed. See Figure 5-22.

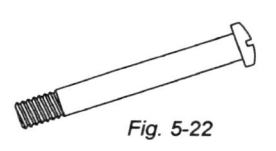

Fig. 5-22

Stirrup and Pin

The stirrup connected the hammer to the main spring. It was a thin, rounded piece of steel 35/64 inches long by 5/64 inches thick with a round crosspiece at the tail which engaged the mainspring's "claws". The crosspiece was 19/64 long by 7/64 inches in diameter. See Figure 5-23.

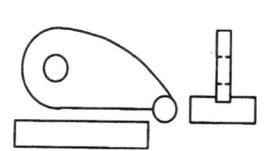

Fig. 5-23

Winchester Lever Action Repeaters

ACTION

The M1892 had a very smooth and tight action. Sloppiness, looseness or conversely a hard or sticky action indicates either excessive wear or incorrect assembly, allowing a part to rub on the interior surface of the receiver. A hard or sticky action can also be caused by shooting the M1892 with cartridges loaded beyond recommended pressures.

Carrier and Carrier Screws

Two types of carriers were produced. The **Type 1** carrier was used on all .25 and .32 caliber M1892s. Its top surface curved upward to a relatively sharp edge on the left side to compensate for the smaller diameter cartridges. The **Type 2** carrier had a flat top surface and was used on all .38 and .44 caliber M1892s. See Figure 5-24. The dashed lines on the side view indicate the additional contours of the .25/.32 carrier.

The carrier incorporated a spring-loaded carrier stop on the left side (arrow). It was held in place by a pin which depended below the top of the carrier. The end of the pin was flush with the top of the carrier so it would not interfere with the loading cycle, but the stop protruded (.25/.32 caliber) 3/32 inches or (.38/44 caliber) 5/32 inches from the side to limit the upward travel of the carrier when the action was opened. The different lengths were required by the fact that the .25/.32 caliber carrier stop detent was on the lower part of the *left cartridge guide* and thus closer to the carrier than on the .38/.44 caliber arms where the carrier stop detent was on the *left inside surface of the receiver wall*, and thus farther away.

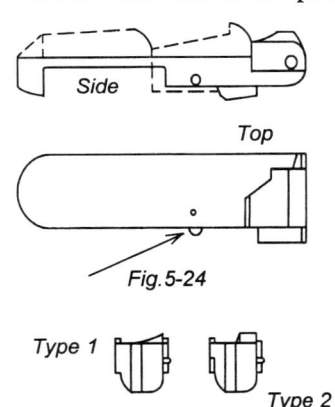

Fig. 5-24

Side / Top / Type 1 / Type 2

Both the Type 1 and Type 2 carriers were 31/64 inches wide at the front expanding to 37/64 inches wide at the rear, by 1 13/32 inches long and 39/64 inches high at the highest point. They had two unthreaded holes, one through each base arm, 1/8 inch forward of the rear edge for the carrier screws.

The Models of 1886 and 1892

NOTE: Although the Type 1 and Type 2 carriers are not interchangeable, they can be "interchangeably installed, i.e., the Type 1 can be installed in the .38 or .44 caliber rifle or carbine and vice-versa, but they will not load cartridges properly. The Type 1 carrier is much more readily available and many .38 and .44 caliber M1892s have been "repaired" with the incorrect Type 1. An incorrect carrier should suggest that a .25 or .32 caliber M1892 may have been converted to a .38 or .44 caliber simply by changing the barrel, which is the only part on which the caliber is marked. The difference in carriers can be seen quite plainly when the action is open.

Two carrier screws were used in the M1892, one on either side of the receiver. They were 3/8 inches long overall. The slotted head was 13/64 inches in diameter by 1/16 inches high. The shank was 3/16 inches in diameter by 5/16 inches long. The center of the shank was threaded 3/16-36, leaving an unthreaded portion, or stud, 5/32 inches in diameter by 7/64 inches long that penetrated the hole in either carrier base arm and served as a pivot. They are identical to and interchangeable with the carrier screws used in the M1894.

Cartridge Guides, Screws and Stops

Two cartridge guides are used to position the cartridge for insertion into the breech, one on either side of the receiver. Both are fastened to the interior of the receiver walls with a single screw. Two types were used, **Type 1** for the .25/.32 caliber receiver and the **Type 2** for the .38/.44 caliber receiver. Dimensions are listed in Table 5-5.

Left Cartridge Guide—.25 and .32 Calibers, Type 1

The *left* cartridge guide was 1 13/16 inches long by 7/8 inches high by 7/32 inches thick. It was milled from a single piece of high-carbon steel. Three holes were bored through the left cartridge guide.

The first was for the cartridge guide screw which was 1/8 inches in diameter and threaded 6-48. It was located 17/32 inches from the rear

Winchester Lever Action Repeaters

TABLE 5-5
M1892 CARTRIDGE GUIDE DIMENSIONS

Description	Type 1 (.25/.32 caliber)		Type 2 (.38/.44 caliber)	
	Left	Right	Left	Right
Length	1 13/16	1 39/64	1 23/32	1 39/64
Thickness	7/32	1/4	7/32	7/32
Height	7/8	5/16	9/16	1/4
Cartridge Guide Screw	Yes	Yes	Yes	Yes
Cartridge Stop Detent	Yes		No	
Cartridge Stop Pin	Yes		Yes	

edge and bored through the side. It was counterbored 1/32 inches deep by 9/32 inches in diameter on the inside surface for the base of the cartridge stop spring, a flat spring with a rounded end. Extending forward from the counterbore is a milled groove 9/64 inches wide by 1 1/64 inches long for the spring's leaf. The groove tapers from 1/32 inches deep at the rear to 3/32 inches at the front. See Figure 5-25A.

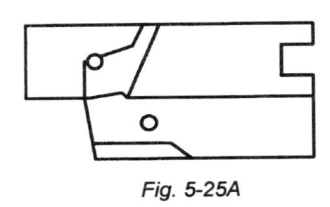

Fig. 5-25A

The second hole was for the carrier stop detent. It was 1/8 inches in diameter and 57/64 inches from the rear. It was unthreaded and served as a detent to limit the upward travel of the carrier.

The Models of 1886 and 1892

The third hole was for the cartridge stop pin. It was drilled from top to bottom, was 1/16 inch in diameter, unthreaded and located 9/64 inches from the front tip of the cartridge guide. The cartridge stop pin secured the cartridge stop to the front of the cartridge guide. The cartridge stop pin was 1/16 inches in diameter and 7/8 inches long.

Left Cartridge Guide — .38 and .44 Calibers, Type 2
The *left* cartridge guide was 1 23/32 inches long by 9/16 inches high by 7/32 inches thick. It was milled from one piece of high-carbon steel. Two holes were bored through the left cartridge guide.

The first was for the cartridge guide screw which was 1/8 inches in diameter and threaded 6-48. It was located 17/32 inches from the rear edge and bored through the side. It was counterbored 1/32 inches deep by 9/32 inches in diameter on the inside surface for the base of the cartridge stop spring, a flat spring with a rounded end. Extending forward from the counterbore was a milled groove 9/64 inches wide by 1 1/64 inches long for the spring's leaf. The groove tapered from 1/32 inches deep at the rear to 3/32 inches at the front. See Figure 5-25B.

The second hole was for the cartridge stop pin. It was drilled from top to bottom, was 1/16 inch in diameter, unthreaded and located 9/64 inches from the front tip of the cartridge guide. The cartridge stop pin secured the cartridge stop to the front of the cartridge guide.

The cartridge stop pin was 1/16 inches in diameter and 7/8 inches long.

Left View

Cartridge Stop Spring
Right view

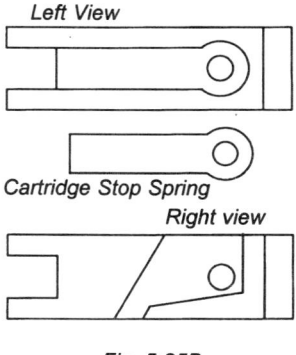

Fig. 5-25B

NOTE: In the .38/.44 caliber receiver, the spring-loaded carrier stop pops into a detent milled into the left inner wall of the receiver, below the cartridge guide, to limit the upward movement of the carrier when the action is opened. Therefore, a third hole was not drilled in the left cartridge guide as it was in the .25/32 caliber cartridge guide.

Winchester Lever Action Repeaters

Right Cartridge Guides

The *right* cartridge guide for the .25/.32 caliber cartridges was also machined from high carbon steel and mounted on the right, inside surface of the receiver near the top of the ejection port. It was 1 39/64 inches long by 5/16 inches high and 1/4 inch thick. It had only one hole 1/8 inches in diameter and threaded 6-48 for the cartridge guide screw. It was located 29/64 inches from the rear edge.

The *right* cartridge guide for the .38/.44 caliber cartridge was machined from high carbon steel and mounted on the right, inside surface of the receiver near the top of the ejection port. It was 1 39/64 inches long by 1/4 inches high and 7/32 inches thick. It had only one hole 1/8 inches in diameter and threaded 6-48 for the cartridge guide screw. It was located 29/64 inches from the rear edge. See Figure 5-26.

NOTE: The Type 1 and Type 2 cartridge guides are interchangeable to a certain extent. The Type 1 cartridge guide will function in either the .25 or .32 caliber receiver. The Type 2 will function in either the .38 or .44 receiver. But the Type 2 (.38/.44) cartridge guide will cause a feeding malfunction if used in the .25/.32 receiver, as will the Type 1 in the .38/.44 caliber receiver.

The cartridge guide screw also secured the cartridge stop spring in its milled groove on the inside surface of the Type 1 and Type 2 left cartridge guide.

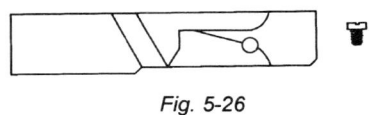

Fig. 5-26

The M1892 cartridge guide screw was identical to and interchangeable with the screw used to mount the M1895 carbine and musket rear sight through the *rear* mounting hole only.

Cartridge Stop

The cartridge stop prevented the next cartridge in the magazine tube from entering the action before the previous cartridge was ejected. Two types of cartridge stops were installed in the M1892. They were

The Models of 1886 and 1892

powered by a cartridge stop spring, described in the Springs section on page 152.

The **Type 1** cartridge stop was used in all .25/.32 caliber receivers. It was 47/64 inches long by 3/8 inches high by 3/16 inches thick, including the slight bulge at the rear which allowed the 5/64 inch cartridge stop pin hole to be drilled. See Figure 5-27A.

The Type 1 has a 1/8 inch by 3/16 inch cutout at the front where the cartridge leaving the magazine tube comes up against the stop. The exact size and shape of the cutout is critical and any modification, intentional or unintentional, will result in misfeeding.

An unthreaded hole was drilled 9/64 inches from the rear of the stop to the center of the hole for the cartridge stop pin. This hole was 1/16 inches in diameter and 11/32 inches long. The cartridge stop pin joined the cartridge stop to the left cartridge guide. The ends of the pin were flush with the top and bottom surfaces of the cartridge guide when properly installed.

The **Type 2** cartridge stop was identical to the Type 1 in all respects except for the cutout at the front. The cutout in the Type 2 is 9/64 inches high by only 3/64 inches deep. See Figure 5-27B.

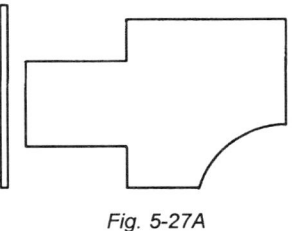

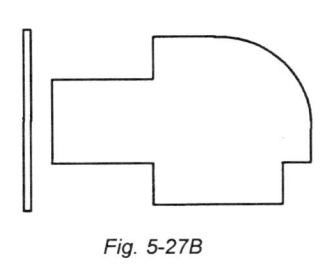

Fig. 5-27A

Fig. 5-27B

Type 1 and Type 2 cartridge stops can be interchanged but will not function properly in the wrong caliber receiver.

Cartridge Guide Screws

The same screw was used for both the Type 1 and Type 2 right and left cartridge guide. It had a slotted, straight-walled, unbeveled

Winchester Lever Action Repeaters

head 3/16 inches in diameter by 3/64 inches high. It was 5/16 inches long and had a 6-48 thread. The cartridge guide screw was inserted through the unthreaded, counterbored hole in the outside surface of the receiver and threaded into the cartridge guide.

Saddle Rings

The M1892 carbine saddle ring and stud was the "U" shaped, double staple-style identical to that used on the M1866 and M1873.

The stud measured 1/4 inches wide at the open end by 11/16 inches high (open end to the bend of the "U"). The diameter of the iron wire was 5/32 inches. A 7/32 inch diameter flange, 5/16 inches from the end of each leg, rested firmly against the receiver wall when properly installed.

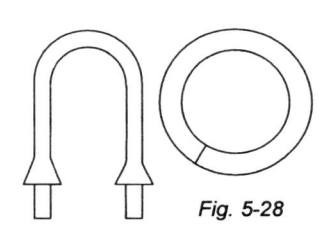

The saddle ring was 1 1/16 inches in outer diameter, 23/32 inches in inner diameter and was made of 11/64 inch diameter iron wire. The ends of the ring were pressed together. Over the years, the ends may have rusted together and give the appearance of having been brazed or welded together. See Figure 5-28.

Fig. 5-28

NOTE: The "Screw-in" type of saddle ring stud found in the M1876, M1886, M1894 and M1895 carbines was never installed on the M1892 carbine.

The Models of 1886 and 1892

BREECHBOLTS

The M1892 breechbolt, although smaller, was quite similar to that used in the M1886. The extractor was mounted in a milled groove on top, the firing pin rode in a tunnel in the center, the ejector, ejector collar and ejector spring were installed inside, below the face of the bolt and the breechbolt was locked into the firing position by two locking bolts, one on either side, that pivoted into grooves cut in the sides of the breechbolt at the rear.

Two types of breechbolts were used on the M1892. They were both 5 5/32 inches long, 3/4 inches high and 27/32 inches wide. The ejector housing protruded 5/32 inches below the bolt body. See Figure 5-29.

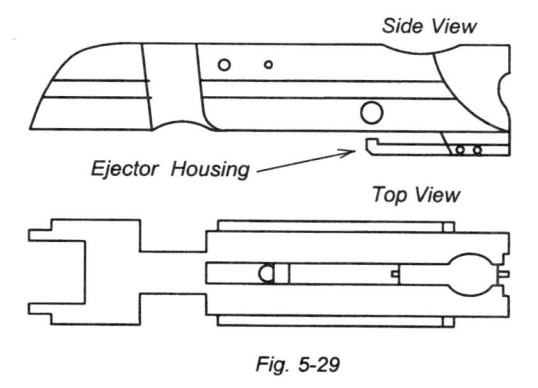

Fig. 5-29

The bolt face for the .25/.32 caliber bolt was smaller at 27/64 inches in diameter than for the .38./44 caliber bolt at 1/2 inch. Therefore, the rim of the .25/.32 cartridge will not fit into the face of the .38/.44 bolt and vice versa. All other dimensions remained the same.

The cutout on the top surface of the breechbolt for the extractor was centered from side to side and was 2 43/64 inches long, 5/32 inches wide and 1/8 inches deep. The extractor cut deepened to 9/32 inches at the rear to accommodate the extractor pin hole stud, then tapered upward to a sharp edge at the rear. An oval-shaped section was milled out near the top front of the breechbolt to allow the extractor to be lubricated. It was 23/64 inches wide by 7/16 inches long.

Winchester Lever Action Repeaters

Channels were milled on either side of the breechbolt, 5/8 inches long by 1/8 inches deep, to receive the left and right hand locking bolts. They were cut at an angle to the rear, 9 degrees from the vertical.

Breechbolts had 1/8 inch high by 7/64 inch wide side rails machined into their right and left sides nearly the full length of the bolt. The rails fitted into corresponding grooves milled into the inside walls of the receiver. These grooves and rails should be lubricated often as they are a friction fit

The M1892 breechbolt had six holes. The **first** was the firing pin tunnel. It was drilled the length of the breech bolt and was 21/64 inches in diameter.

The **second** hole was for the finger lever and breechbolt pin. It was located 1 3/16 inches behind the bolt face. It was 3/16 inches in diameter and unthreaded.

The breechbolt pin was 11/64 inches in diameter, 19/32 inches long and made of case-hardened steel. The 1/64 inch difference in size between the hole and pin diameter allowed the pin to rotate freely and serve as a pivot for the finger lever. It was polished flat on one end but beveled 1/64 inch on the other to aid in installation. The flat above the bevel was 9/64 inches in diameter.

NOTE: A sticky action in a M1892 may be due to the wrong size or improperly installed lever and breechbolt pin, or one that has been removed by hammering. Check for scoring of the receiver wall and damaged ends on the pin. Because of the close fit between bolt and receiver, any part of the pin protruding beyond the bolt's surface will rub on the receiver wall.

The **third** hole was for the extractor pin, near the top of the bolt 1 29/32 inches behind the face. The hole was 3/32 inches in diameter.

The Models of 1886 and 1892

The extractor pin was 3/32 inches in diameter by 37/64 inches long and was press-fitted into the hole in the bolt to retain the extractor. The ends of the pin were flush with the sides of the breechbolt. See Figure 5-30.

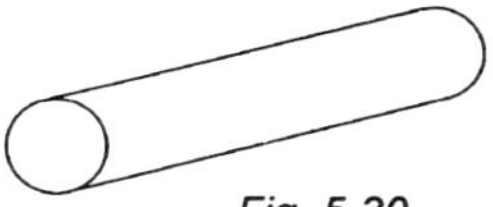

The **fourth** hole was for the firing pin stop pin. It was 2 29/64 inches behind the face of the breechbolt and was 1/8 inches in diameter.

Fig. 5-30

The firing pin stop pin retained the firing pin in the breechbolt. The firing pin stop pin was 1/8 inches in diameter by 37/64 inches long. It passed through both sides of the breechbolt and through a milled cutout in the firing pin long enough to allow the firing pin to move back so that the tip did not rest on the cartridge primer.

The **fifth** and **sixth** holes held the ejector assembly retainer in the breechbolt. Both were drilled across the width, near the bottom of the breechbolt, 5/16 and 35/64 inches respectively behind the face. Both were 3/32 inches in diameter.

NOTE: The ejector assembly retainer may be a permanent machined part, or secured with only one pin in the bolt. The author suspects that Winchester had a great deal of trouble with this part breaking. They first tried—without success—to solve the problem with a single pin. When this did not work, a second pin was added. Early serial numbered M1892s with two pins may well have been returned to the factory for repair. This was accomplished by milling off the old retainer and installing the new one with two pins.

The collector should always check to make certain that the entire ejector assembly is present, that the extractor is functional and that the firing pin tip is not broken. Missing or broken breechbolt parts are difficult and expensive to replace, and will lower the value of a M1892 considerably. Only three simple tests are required:

Winchester Lever Action Repeaters

1) Press on the front of the *ejector* where it protrudes past the bolt face. If it moves to the rear, then springs back immediately with considerable force, it is satisfactory and correctly installed.

2) View the extractor from above, Make certain that it is installed on the upper surface of the breechbolt and is not cracked or broken throughout its length. Reach into the face of the breechbolt and check the flange or hook on the inside that rides over the cartridge rim to make certain that it is intact and not broken off. Replacement extractors are expensive.

3) Test the firing pin by pushing it from the rear to force it to protrude from the breechbolt face. If the tip does not appear, it has broken off. If the tip appears, draw the firing pin to the rear again. If the rear of the firing pin withdraws but the tip does not, it is broken along its length.

Locking Bolts
Two rectangular pieces of steel milled to shape were moved upward by the finger lever into two grooves, one on either side, to lock the bolt to the receiver when in battery. No changes were made to the locking bolts during M1892 production.

The locking bolts were 37/64 inches wide by 2 13/64 inches long by 7/32 inches thick. Both had a groove milled in the inside back surface 1/8 inches wide by 1 1/32 inches long by 3/64 inches deep. When the locking bolts moved up and down, they were guided by these grooves which pressed against the forward protruding edges of the lower tang. The locking bolts should always be kept lubricated to insure a smooth working action and to prevent wear.

The M1892 locking bolts had a 1/4 inch diameter unthreaded hole 19/32 inches above the bottom edge of the locking bolt and 15/64 inches behind the front edge for the locking bolt pin linking the finger lever to the locking bolts.

The Models of 1886 and 1892

The *left* locking bolt had a second hole 19/64 inches from the front edge and 13/32 inches above the bottom. It was 1/8 inches in diameter, drilled through and counterbored to 9/32 inches. It was threaded 6-48 for the locking bolt pin stop screw. The counterbore permitted the screw to fit flush with the locking bolt so that it did not rub against the receiver wall. The counterbore also overlapped the locking pin hole so that the head of the locking bolt pin stop screw fitted into a cut 9/64 inch long by 3/64 inch deep milled in the head of the locking bolt pin. See Figure 5-31.

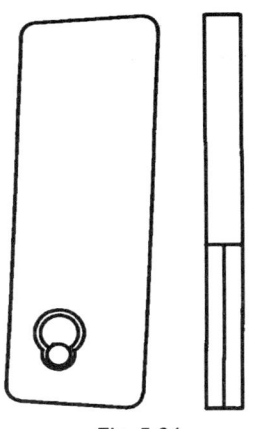

Fig. 5-31

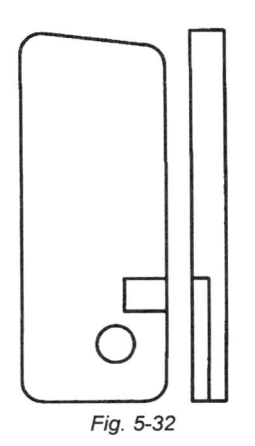

The *left* locking bolt pin hole was counterbored. This allowed the head of the locking bolt pin to fit flush with the outer surface of the locking bolt and not rub against the receiver wall. The *right* locking bolt pin hole was not counterbored.

The *right* locking bolt had an additional 5/16 inch high by 15/64 inch long slot milled in the outer surface just above the locking bolt pin hole to allow the loading gate to pivot inward. It tapered from 0 inches to 3/32 inches deep, rear to front. See Figure 5-32.

Fig. 5-32

Locking Bolt Pin

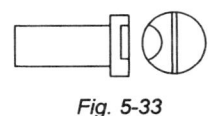

The locking bolt pin connected the left and right locking bolts with the finger lever. It was 1/4 inches in diameter by 25/32 inches long. It had a head 17/64 inches in diameter by 3/32 inches high. The head of the pin rested in the countebored hole in the left locking bolt so that it was flush with its surface. See Figure 5-33.

Fig. 5-33

145

Winchester Lever Action Repeaters

The locking bolt pin had a screwdriver slot cut across the head so that a screwdriver could be used to align it properly for the locking bolt pin stop screw to be inserted.

The locking bolt pin had a 9/64 inch long by 3/64 inch deep cutout milled in the head of the locking bolt pin. When turned into proper alignment, the locking bolt pin stop screw fitted down into the cutout to prevent the locking bolt pin from backing out.

Locking Bolt Pin Stop Screw
The locking bolt pin stop screw's function was to secure the locking bolt pin in place and prevent it from backing out. It threaded down in a counterbored screw hole at the 5 o'clock position on the locking bolt in relation to the pin hole, and its head filled the 9/64 inch long by 3/64 inch deep milled cutout on the head of the locking bolt pin. When properly installed, it was flush with the surface of the locking bolt. See Figure 5-34.

The locking bolt pin stop screw was 13/64 inches long. Its head was 17/64 inches in diameter and 3/64 inches high. Its shank was 9/64 inches in diameter and threaded 6-48.

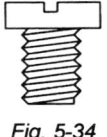

Fig. 5-34

NOTE: When reassembling the action, take care to align the locking bolt pin using the screwdriver slot so that the locking bolt pin stop screw can be tightened all the way down with its head flush with the locking bolt surface. Otherwise, the locking bolt pin stop screw's head will rub against the inside of the receiver, making the action difficult to work.

Extractor
Two types of extractors were used in the M1892 to pull the fired case from the breech. Both types of extractor had a 7/64 inch diameter unthreaded hole for the extractor pin which held the extractor into the milled groove in the top of the breechbolt. Both types of extractors

The Models of 1886 and 1892

were made of spring steel, and were 9/64 inches wide by 1 51/64 inches long and 7/64 inches thick except for the mounting pin hole stud where it was 7/32 inches thick. See Figure 5-35.

The **Type 1** extractor was installed in the .25 and .32 caliber breechbolts. Its claw was 9/64 inches high by 15/64 inches long and its pinhole was 2 inches from the front..

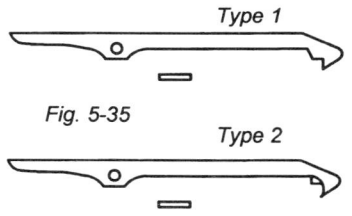

Fig. 5-35

The **Type 2** extractor was installed in the .38 and .44 caliber breechbolts. Its claw was 3/32 inches high by 3/32 inches long and its pinhole was 1 63/64 inches from the front.

The extractor pin was 3/32 inches in diameter by 9/16 inches long.

NOTE: The M1892 Type 2 .38/.44 caliber extractor was completely interchangeable with all extractors used on the M1894, regardless of caliber.

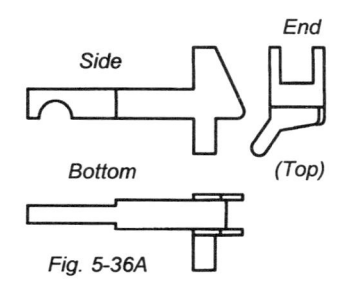

Ejector Assembly

The ejector assembly used on the M1892 consisted of the ejector, collar and spring. All parts were made of steel and blued. The ejector was 1 9/16 inches long overall, 7/64 inches wide at the rear and 1/4 inches wide at the front. The slot for the lever and breech bolt pin which retained the ejector was milled on the bottom of the ejector body and was 11/32 inches long by 1/16 inches deep. See Figure 5-36A.

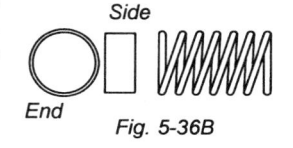

Fig. 5-36A

Fig. 5-36B

The ejector collar had an outside diameter of 1/4 inches and an inside diameter of 5/32 inches. It was 11/64 inches long. See Figure 5-36B.

Winchester Lever Action Repeaters

The ejector spring was made from round steel wire 1/32 inches in diameter. It had five coils and an outside diameter of 15/64 inches. It was approximately 25/32 inches long. Refer to Figure 5-36B.

Firing Pin

Only one type of firing pin was manufactured. It was 3 19/32 inches long by 9/32 inches in diameter at the rear. The tip was 19/64 inches long by 3/32 inches in diameter. All firing pins were blued. See Figure 5-36C.

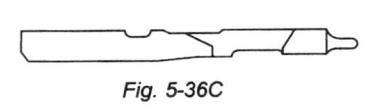

Fig. 5-36C

Finger Lever

Only two types of finger levers were used throughout the M1892 production run, regardless of caliber or other variation. Both had the spring and plunger lever catch similar to that used on the M1886, but located on the rear top surface of the trigger loop, rather than the front, as with the M1886.

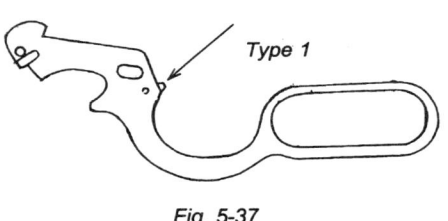

Type 1

Fig. 5-37

The **Type 1** finger lever was straight and used on all standard, non-pistol grip stocked rifles and carbines. It was 23/64 inches wide by 7 13/16 inches long by 2 1/4 inches high at its highest point. The loop was an oval with an inside diameter of 2 31/64 inches long by 49/64 inches high. The loop was 1/8 inch thick and made of casehardened steel. See Figure 5-37.

The **Type 2** finger lever was curved to match the curve of the pistol-grip lower tang. It was 23/64 inches wide, 7 23/64 inches long by 51/64 inches high at the center. See Figure 5-38A.

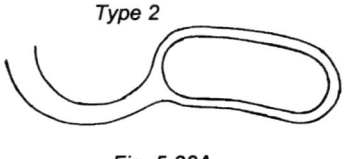

Type 2

Fig. 5-38A

The Models of 1886 and 1892

Three holes were drilled through the finger lever. The *first* was 3/16 inches in diameter and 1/4 inch behind the front edge. This unthreaded hole was used to attached the lever to the breechbolt with the lever and breechbolt pin.

The *second* hole was an oval-shaped cutout 17/64 inches wide by 29/64 inches long. It was 1 59/64 inches behind the front edge. The locking bolt pin passed through this hole to attach the finger lever to the locking bolts.

The oval-shaped cutout had two purposes: 1) to allow the finger lever to be lowered far enough to allow the lever and breechbolt pin to pull the firing pin away from the cartridge primer slightly before the locking bolts descended. 2) As the action was closed, the oval-shaped cutout allowed the locking bolts to rise completely to lock the breechbolt shut before the firing pin was cammed forward, thus preventing the gun from firing before the action was fully closed.

The *third* hole was 7/64 inches in diameter and was positioned 2 15/32 inches behind the front of the lever. It housed the friction stud stop pin which retained the friction stud and spring. The hole was unthreaded. The friction stud stop pin was press-fitted into the lever.

Friction Stud, Spring and Stop Pin

The friction stud (see Figure 5-38b) included a spring-loaded plunger set into the finger lever above the trigger bow (arrow, Fig. 5-37). The plunger was 1/4 inch in diameter by 19/32 inches long with a notch in its upper surface 11/64 inches wide for the friction stud stop pin. The friction stud stop pin was 7/64 inches in diameter and 11/32 inches long. It was polished flush with the side of the finger lever. The friction stud spring was made of steel wire 1/64 inches in diameter wound into 5 coils 13/64 inches in diameter.

Figure 5-38B

Winchester Lever Action Repeaters

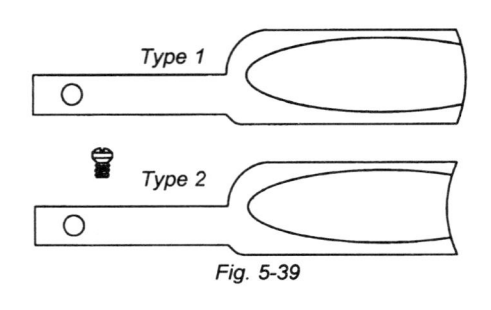

Loading Gate

Winchester called this part the "spring cover," but today's users normally refer to it as the loading gate. The M1892 returned to the familiar one-piece spring steel loading gate used on all previous models except for the M1886—and the M1895—which lacked a loading gate.

Fig. 5-39

The M1892 loading gate (see Figure 5-39) was 2 1/2 inches long. The forward part covering the loading port was 1 3/64 inches long, 1/2 inch high and 5/64 inches thick. The tang was 29/64 inches long, 15/64 inches high and 1/32 inches thick. A 1/8 inch diameter hole 5/16 inches from the rear edge was drilled through the tang and threaded 6-48 for the loading gate screw.

The loading gate screw had a slotted head 3/16 inches in diameter and beveled shoulders. It was 9/64 inches long overall and had a 6-48 thread. It passed through the receiver wall from the outside and threaded into the loading gate tang.

Two types of loading gates were used, and cannot be interchanged without modification. The **Type 1** loading gate was installed in the .25 and .32 caliber M1892 receivers and the **Type 2** in the .38 and .44 caliber receivers.

The leading edge of the **Type 1** loading gate curved slightly toward the muzzle and protruded outward 1/64 inches. The **Type 2** loading gate curved slightly to the rear and had a cutout 1/32 inches long to accommodate the larger rims of the .38-40 and .44-40 cartridges.

Mainspring

The mainspring used in the M1892 was the same design as used in the M1873 and M1894. But it can also be installed in the M1866, M1876

The Models of 1886 and 1892

and M1886 even though those models did not require the hole at the rear for the mainspring screw. See Figure 5-40.

The mainspring was 3 15/32 inches long when measured along the inner curve and 3 33/64 inches long when measured around the outer curve. It was 3/8 inches wide at the base but tapered to 21/64 inches wide at the front, or claw end and had a double hook, or claw, 1/4 inches long by 1/16 inches deep. The claw engaged the hammer stirrup and secured it to the hammer.

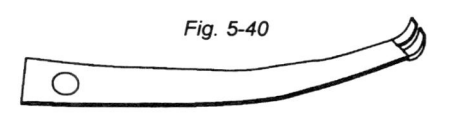

Fig. 5-40

The M1892 mainspring had a single hole 1/4 inch forward of the rear edge. The hole was 11/64 inches in diameter and was threaded 9-32 for the mainspring screw which secured it to the inside upper surface of the lower tang.

The mainspring screw had a slotted head 1/4 inches in diameter and 9/64 inches high. The screw was 31/64 inches long. The shank was 11/32 inches long and had a 9-32 thread, 7/32 inches from the bottom.

The mainspring screw was inserted through the lower tang and threaded into the mainspring.

The mainspring tension, regulating the degree of force with which the hammer struck, was adjusted via a mainspring tension screw just forward of the mainspring screw. It was a slotted screw 17/64 inches long and threaded 9-32 the length of the shank. It screwed into a hole drilled in the bottom of the lower tang and pressed against the mainspring. The head was 13/64 inches in diameter and 1/32 inches high. The shank was 11/64 inches in diameter. The screw was designed to bottom out in the counterbored hole to prevent excessive pressure being applied to the spring.

Winchester Lever Action Repeaters

Trigger Spring

The trigger spring was made of flat spring steel stock 1/16 inches thick at the base near the mounting screw hole, tapering to 1/64 inches thick at the bearing end. It was 5/16 inches wide at the rear but tapered to 9/32 inches wide at the bearing end. Overall, the spring was 1 19/32 inches long. See Figure 5-41.

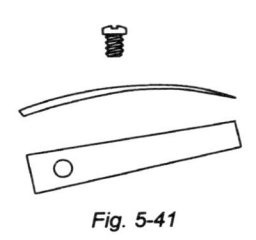

Fig. 5-41

A hole 9/64 inches in diameter was bored through the spring 13/64 inches from the end for the trigger spring screw.

The trigger spring screw had a head 13/64 inches in diameter and 1/16 inches high. The shank was 1/8 inches in diameter by 1/4 inches long and threaded 6-48. It was inserted from inside the tang, passed through the base of the trigger spring and screwed into the lower tang. The exterior end of this screw had the appearance of a pin when viewed from the outside.

Cartridge Stop Spring

The cartridge stop spring was mounted between the left cartridge guide and the left side of the receiver and held in place by the left cartridge guide screw. It pivoted the cartridge stop into the magazine tube opening to prevent the following cartridge from entering the receiver until the first cartridge was inserted in the chamber. See Figure 5-42.

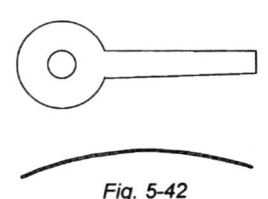

Fig. 5-42

It was a small, thin leaf spring 1/8 inches wide by 1 3/16 inches long and 1/64 inches thick. It had a 5/32 inch diameter hole in its circular base by which it was mounted to the left cartridge guide.

The Models of 1886 and 1892

Forends and Forearms

Rifle forends and carbine forearms for the M1892 were made of straight grain American walnut. Dimensions are shown below in Table 5-6 and the rifle and carbine forend and forearms are shown in Figures 5-43 and 5-44.

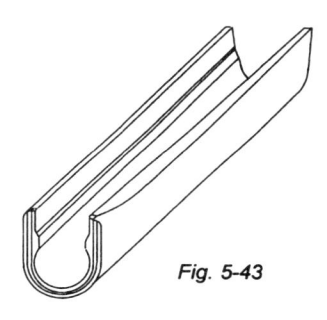

M1892 forends installed on .38/.44 caliber rifles will interchange with M1894 rifle *forends*. But M1894 rifle forend magazine tube tunnel is too large for the .25/.32 caliber magazine tube.

Fig. 5-43

NOTE: Throughout production, Winchester had trouble obtaining supplies of suitable walnut and often substituted "gumwood" which was softer than, and lacked walnut's attractive grain. Gumwood was used almost exclusively on carbines to reduce weight. Gumwood forends were never installed on rifles as the lighter wood allowed the center of gravity to move forward, making the rifle muzzle-heavy. Gumwood can often be identified by its dark, even surface coloring and dented appearance. Gumwood stocks lower the collector's value of a M1892 Winchester lever action carbine or rifle.

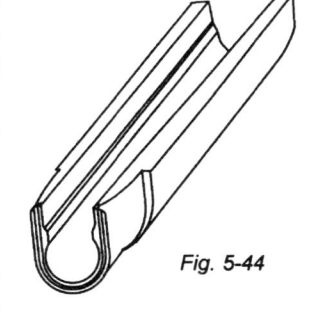

Trapper or Baby Carbine Forearms

Carbine forearms 8 1/8 inches long were installed on about one-half of all "Trapper" or "Baby" carbines with less than 15 inch length barrels. The standard length carbine forearm was installed on the remainder and will predominate on those with barrel lengths of 16, 17, 18 or 19 inches. The author has never observed the shorter carbine forearm on a carbine with an 18 inch or longer barrel.

Fig. 5-44

Winchester Lever Action Repeaters

To identify the 8 1/8 inch carbine forearm as original, look for the following points: 1) the barrel band will have protected the wood beneath, leaving a lighter colored, dent-free area. 2) The barrel band increased in thickness toward the muzzle. A forearm that has been cut back may show a gap at the front of the barrel band and a very tight fit at the rear. To correct this, some wood may have been removed. 3) The rear of the forearm may show a rough cut and may not fit the receiver as closely as an original forearm. 4) Wood will have been removed to produce the 3/32 inch step that fits into the front of the receiver. Look for chisel and saw marks. 5) Measure the length. It should be exactly 8 1/8 inches ± 1/16 inches. Always keep in mind that Winchester workers hand-fitted each forearm perfectly.

Forend Tips

Three types of forend tips were installed on the M1892 rifle. Their overall dimensions were the same, 1 3/64 inches wide by 1 1/64 inches long and 1 11/64 inches high, but the size of the magazine tube opening differed. The standard M1892 forend tip was blued. Forend tips were finished in color case-hardening only on special order, and almost always in conjunction with a color case-hardened receiver. See Figure 5-45.

The **Type 1** forend tip used on the .25/.32 caliber rifle had a magazine tube opening 35/64 inches in diameter. It was not interchangeable with those used on the M1894 as the magazine tube opening was too small.

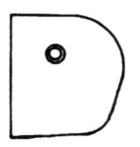

Fig. 5-45

The **Type 2** forend tip for the .38/.44 caliber rifles had a magazine tube opening 21/32 inches in diameter. It was interchangeable with those used on the M1894 rifle.

The Models of 1886 and 1892

TABLE 5-6
MODEL 1892 FOREND AND FOREARM DIMENSIONS
(INCHES—ALL VARIANCE, 1/16 INCHES)

PART	LENGTH	HEIGHT BREECH	HEIGHT MUZZLE	WIDTH BREECH	WIDTH MUZZLE	MAGAZINE TUBE TUNNEL DIAMETER
Rifle .38/44 caliber	9 3/8	1 7/16	1 11/64	1 9/32	1 1/16	21/32
Rifle .25/.32 caliber	9 3/8	1 7/16	1 11/64	1 9/32	1 1/16	35/64
Rifle Takedown .38/.44	9 3/8	1 7/16	1 11/16	1 9/32	1 1/16	3/4
Rifle Takedown .25/.32	9 3/8	1 7/16	1 11/16	1 9/32	1 1/16	41/64[1]
Carbine[2] .38/.44	9 1/8	1 15/16	29/32	1 9/32	63/64	21/32
Carbine[2] .25/.32	9 1/8	1 15/16	29/32	1 9/32	63/64	35/64
Carbine, Trapper's[3]	8 1/8	1 15/16	29/32	1 9/32	63/64	21/32 (.38/.44) 35/64 (.25/.32)

1 The diameter remains constant for 45/64 inches to accommodate the magazine tube guide on the front face of the takedown extension
2 Carbine forearms are 1 3/16 inches wide at rear of barrel band and 1 5/64 inches wide at front. They are 1 15/16 inches high at rear of barrel band and 1 7/32 inches high at front. All variances are 1/16 inches.
3 Length varies according to barrel length and other factors. See "Trapper or Baby Carbine" section below.

Winchester Lever Action Repeaters

NOTE: Both the Type 1 and Type 2 forend tips were used on those rifles with full or "fractional" length magazines only.

The Type 1 and 2 forend tips had a 1/8 inch diameter hole, countersunk to 7/32 inches in diameter, on either side for the forend tip screws. The holes were located 27/64 inches ahead of the rear edge. The forend tip screws passed through these holes and threaded into the forend tip tenon held to the bottom of the barrel in a dovetail. The screw heads were flush with the outer surface of the tip when properly installed.

The forend tip screws were 1/4 inch long. Their slotted heads were 13/64 inches in diameter and 5/64 inches high. The shank was 11/64 inches long and threaded 6-48 along its length. See Figure 5-46.

Fig. 5-46

Type 3 Forend Tips for "Button Magazine" Rifles

This type of forend tip was used on special order rifles in which the magazine tube was completely enclosed within the forearm. Only the rounded magazine end plug protruded slightly past the forend tip. Dimensions were the same as for the Type 1 and 2—1 3/64 inches wide by 1 1/64 inches long and 1 11/64 inches high—with the exception of the magazine end plug openings. See Figure 5-47.

The magazine end plug opening for the .25/.32 caliber Type 3 forend tip was 15/32 inches in diameter; it was 9/16 inches in diameter for the .38/.44 caliber variations.

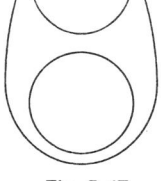

Fig. 5-47

The magazine tube opening for the Type 3 Button Magazine Forend cap formed a complete circle, whereas the magazine tube opening for the Type 1 and Type 2 forend tips formed a partial circle open at the top, just under the barrel.

The Models of 1886 and 1892

Forend Tip Tenon

The forend tip tenon was a rectangular piece of steel 29/32 inches wide by 3/8 inches long by 9/32 inches high. It fitted into a dovetail 3/8 inches long milled into the bottom of the barrel just forward of the forend. See Figure 5-48.

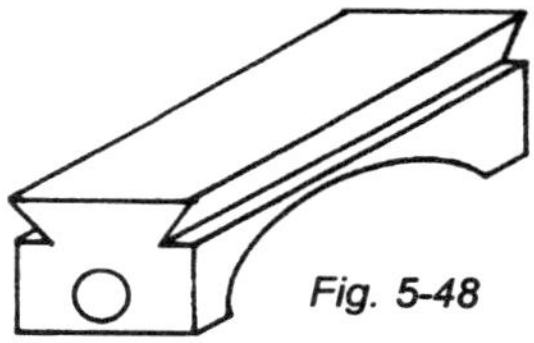

Fig. 5-48

The rifle forend tip was attached to the forend tip tenon by the forend tip screws. Their dimensions are given above in the section describing the Type 1 and 2 forend tips.

Winchester Lever Action Repeaters

Barrels

The standard rifle and carbine barrel was round. Octagonal rifle barrels were available on special order. As the octagonal barrel was still considered to be stronger than the round barrel as late as the turn of the 20th Century, the octagonal barrel will predominate on early rifles. See Figure 5-49.

The standard rifle barrel length was 24 inches and the standard carbine barrel was 20 inches. The actual length of the barrel was almost always slightly longer than specified in the catalog. Table 5-7 provides barrel dimensions.

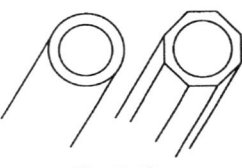

Fig. 5-49

Longer or shorter than standard barrels could be ordered until about 1908, but were not ordered in large quantities. After 1908, shorter than standard barrels could still be special ordered. Carbines with barrels shorter than the standard 20 inches are generally referred to by collectors as "trapper" or "baby" carbines.

Takedown barrels are the same as fixed barrels with the exception of the interrupted threads on either side of the shank to enable the barrel to be turned 90 degrees counter-clockwise and removed. See Figure 5-50.

NOTE: M1892 barrels had a tendency to develop a ring in the bore under the front sight. This gave rise to the belief that the gun would be more accurate if the barrel were cut off behind this ring. Check carefully to see that the barrel has not been shortened for this reason as it will greatly reduce the collector's value of the firearm. This same theory was also applied to the carbine.

Fig. 5-50

The Models of 1886 and 1892

TABLE 5-7
M1892 BARREL DIMENSIONS
(INCHES)

TYPE	CROSS SECTION	CATALOG LENGTH	ACTUAL LENGTH	WIDTH AT BREECH	WIDTH AT MUZZLE
Rifle	Round	24	24 1/4 ± 3/8	7/8 ± 3/64	11/16 ± 1/32
Rifle	Octagon	24	24 5/16 ± 1/8	27/32 ± 3/64	23/32 ± 1/32
Rifle	Rapid Taper	24	24 1/8 ± 3/8	57/64 ± 3/64	35/64 ± 1/32
Carbine	Round- to circa 250,000	20	19 7/8 to 19 15/16	15/16 ± 3/64	19/32 ± 1/32
Carbine	Round- after circa 250,000	20	20 1/32 ± 7/32	59/64 ± 3/64	19/32 ± 1/32

Barrel Rifling

All M1892 barrels had 6 lands and grooves.

From the start of production to circa serial #390,000, the rifling twist rate for all rifle barrels in all calibers was 1:30 with the grooves one-quarter wider than the lands.

From circa serial #390,000-675,000, the rifling twist rate for all rifle barrels in all calibers was 1:24 and the grooves were three-quarters wider than the lands.

From circa serial #675,000 to the end of production, the rifling twist rate for all rifle barrels in all calibers was 1:36 and the grooves were one-quarter wider than the lands.

Winchester Lever Action Repeaters

Carbine barrels in .38 and .44 caliber followed that same rifling pattern as for the rifle barrels throughout production.

Throughout production, .25 caliber carbine barrels had a rifling twist rate of 1:20 and the grooves were twice as wide as the lands.

Throughout production, .32 caliber carbine barrels had a rifling twist rate of 1:24 and the grooves were one-quarter wider than the lands.

Barrel Crowns

The standard rifle barrel was uncrowned, finished flat and polished across the muzzle. A *few* lightweight rifles with the 22 inch rapid taper barrel were crowned, however.

All carbine barrels were crowned. The crown measured 1/32 inches high. See Figure 5-51.

NOTE: M1892 barrels had a tendency to develop a ring in the bore under the front sight. This gave rise to the belief that the gun would be more accurate if the barrel was cut off behind this ring. Check carefully to see that the barrel has not been shortened for this reason as it will greatly reduce the collector's value of the firearm. This same theory was also applied to the rifle.

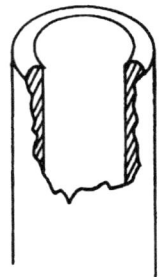

Fig. 5-51

Dovetails

All dovetails cut into Model 1892 barrels were 3/8 inches long, with the exception of that for the magazine tube ring which was really an elliptically cut slot, rather than a dovetail. See Figure 5-52.

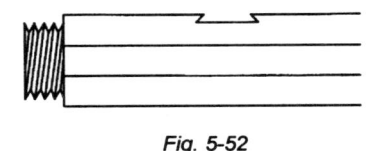

Fig. 5-52

The rear sight dovetail on the *rifle* barrel was located 4 3/4 to 4 7/8 ahead

The Models of 1886 and 1892

of the receiver to the rear of the dovetail slot.

The rear sight dovetail on the *carbine* barrel was located 2 3/16 to 2 5/16 from the front edge of the receiver to the rear of the dovetail slot. For those carbines fitted with the semi-buckhorn rifle-type rear sight, the dovetail was cut 2 13/16 to 2 15/16 from the front edge of the receiver to the rear of the dovetail slot.

All .25 and .32 caliber carbine barrels used a magazine tube ring rather than a barrel band as on the .38 and .44 caliber carbines. The recoil from these light cartridges did not dislodge the magazine tube. The magazine tube slots on all .25 and .32 caliber carbines were cut 3 25/32 ± 1/16 inches behind the muzzle end of the barrel.

The magazine tube ring slot on takedown variations was located 3 to 3 1/2 inches behind the muzzle to the front edge of the slot. See Table 5-8 for exact measurements.

TABLE 5-8
M1892 RECEIVER FACE TO MAGAZINE TUBE SLOT DISTANCES
(INCHES)

24 inch Barrel Rifle	19 1/2 ± 1/16 to rear of magazine tube slot
26 inch Barrel Rifle	21 15/32 ± 1/16 to rear of magazine tube slot
20 inch Barrel .25/.32 Carbine	15 1/2 ± 1/16 to rear of magazine tube slot
24 inch Barrel Takedown Rifles	18 25/32 to 19 7/32 to rear of magazine tube slot
26 inch Barrel Takedown Rifles	20 3/4 to 21 3/16 to rear of magazine tube slot

Winchester Lever Action Repeaters

NOTE: These measurements can be used to help determine whether or not the magazine tube ring slot has been recut or the barrel shortened.

Barrel Markings

Winchester name and address markings were roll-die marked on the top or side of *rifle* barrels in front of the rear sight dovetail. On *carbines*, the markings were roll-die marked on the top between the rear barrel band and the rear sight dovetail.

A total of five different barrel address markings are found on the M1892 rifle and carbine. The collector should be aware of the following caveats regarding M1892 barrel markings.

1. If a marking is found on a barrel that is inconsistent with the standard marking of that serial number range, it does not necessarily mean the barrel has been changed or the marking altered. Winchester used worn roll dies long after they had been replaced with newer ones as a matter of economy. The transition from one style of marking to another may encompass literally thousands of serial numbers. It is also entirely possible that one worker charged with marking barrels, rather than wait for another worker to finish using a particular roll die, simply used whatever die was available, rather than waste the time waiting. At this period, many Winchester workers were still paid piece-rates. This could explain why most older roll die markings found in the serial number range of a newer marking almost always appear lightly impressed and with broken letters.

2. When a new or current die broke, an older die was often pressed into service while a replacement die was being made. This would account for minor differences in markings within a specific serial number range, such as different spacing between letters and words, the use of periods instead of commas and vice-versa and the differing length of dashes, as well the lines themselves.

The Models of 1886 and 1892

3.   The collector can assure him or herself that these are correct Winchester markings by examining them closely to make certain that they are *stamped* into the metal and not *engraved* (engraved letters and numbers will show very sharp edges and slight curls or scallops in the channels where the metal was cut away. Stamped letters and numbers will show a slight ridge of harder, lighter-colored metal around the periphery and smooth channels rounded at the bottom). The collector should also look for the double proof mark usually associated with a repair performed at the Winchester factory.

4.   Make certain that the condition of the barrel matches that of the rest of the rifle or carbine.

The **Type 1** barrel address marking was used from the start of production to circa serial #200,000:

**MANUFACTURED BY THE
—WINCHESTER REPEATING ARMS CO. NEW HAVEN, CONN. U.S.A.—**

The letters were in capitals without serifs. The first line was 1 7/32 inches long and the letters were 5/64 inches high. The second line was preceded and ended by dashes. It was 3 7/32 inches long and the letters were 5/64 inches high.

The **Type 2** barrel address marking was in use from circa serial #200,000-250,000:

**MANUFACTURED BY THE WINCHESTER REPEATING ARMS CO.
——— NEW HAVEN, CONN. U.S.A. PAT. OCT.14, 1884 ———**

The letters were in capitals without serifs but with well-defined commas. The first line was 3 19/32 inches long and the letters were 5/64 inches high. The second line was 3 7/32 inches long and the letters were 5/64 inches high. Long dashes were used to make the second line almost as long as the first. The gap between the dashes and the nearest letter was 3/64 inches.

Winchester Lever Action Repeaters

The **Type 3** barrel address marking was in use from circa serial #250,000-350,000:

—MANUFACTURED BY THE—
—WINCHESTER REPEATING ARMS CO. NEW HAVEN. CONN. U.S.A.—

The letters were in capitals without serifs. The first line was 1 7/8 inches long and the letters were 3/32 inches high. The dashes at the end of the first line were 3/16 inches long. The second line was 4 inches long and the letters were also 3/32 inches high. The dashes at the end of the second line were 5/32 inches long. The punctuation marks after the abbreviated words appear to be periods rather than commas, although this may also be the effect of die wear.

The **Type 4** barrel address marking was used circa serial #350,000-900,000:

MANUFACTURED BY THE WINCHESTER REPEATING ARMS CO.
NEW HAVEN, CONN. U.S.A. PATENTED   OCTOBER   14,   1884

The letters were in capitals without serifs. Both lines were 2 3/4 inches long and the letters were 5/64 inches high. The unusual spacing has never been explained. There appears to be almost no spacing between the period following "CONN" and the letter "U" and again between the period following "A" and the word "PATENTED". Then, as if to make up for the spacing "error", double spaces were added between "PATENTED" and "OCTOBER", again between "OCTOBER" and "14", and again between the comma following "14" and "1884".

The **Type 5** barrel address marking appeared at circa serial #900,000. It was roll die marked on the left side of the barrel between the rear sight dovetail and the left top edge of the forend or forearm:

MADE IN NEW HAVEN, CONN. U.S. OF AMERICA
—— WINCHESTER PROOF STEEL ——

The Models of 1886 and 1892

The letters were in capitals without serifs. Both lines were 2 13/32 inches long and the letters were 3/32 inches high. The barrel address was immediately followed (in the direction of the breech) by the marking:

—WINCHESTER—
— TRADE MARK —

The first line was Winchester's new stylized logotype in italics with serifs. The second line was in non-serif, block type. Both lines were 1 11/32 inches long. The letters in the first line were 9/64 inches high, but only 5/64 inches high in the second line.

Caliber Markings

Caliber markings were between 3/4 and 7/8 inches long, depending on the number of letters and numbers required. The model and caliber markings were struck on the barrel immediately following the Winchester address and trade mark. If the address marking was on the top of the barrel, so was the caliber marking; if the address marking was on the side, so was the caliber marking.

—MODEL 92 — 44 W.C.F—

The line was 1 15/16 inches long and the letters and numbers were without serifs and 5/32 inches high. This type of marking, with the exception of the model designator, was also used on the continuation Model 53.

Barrel Markings—Trapper/Baby Carbines

Barrels longer than 16 inches will show the standard barrel markings. On those shorter than 16 inches, the barrel marking was as often roll die marked in front of the rear barrel band, as it was in the standard location. Address marking placement on short barrels seems to have been left to the individual assembler.

Winchester Lever Action Repeaters

NOTE: When assessing the originality of a "trapper/baby" carbine, look for evidence of cut barrels, cut magazine tubes, front sights that have been moved and recut magazine tube ring slots, rather than location of barrel markings or the length of the forearm, as these will vary too widely. Keep in mind that it is very difficult to duplicate these metal cuts without the same machinery that Winchester used and the skills of its workers. Evidence of forgery will almost always be apparent, if you look for it.

Barrel Proof Mark

The Winchester proof mark, the stylized W/P as shown in Figure 5-53, is seen only on barrels installed on the M1892 after circa 1905. The presence or absence of the proof mark on barrels originally installed at the factory has little bearing on the collector's value of the rifle or carbine.

Fig. 5-53

The collector should be aware that Winchester Lever Actions returned to the factory after circa 1905 for barrel replacement or repairs, may have had the Winchester proof mark added. In such cases, the value of the firearm would be reduced, reflecting the fact that the barrel was no longer original.

Stainless Steel Barrels

A few M1892 barrels were made of stainless steel. They can be distinguished in two ways. First, stainless steel will not accept a blued (oxidized) finish and so they were "jappaned". Japan was a bitumen-derived varnish that was painted on and fixed by heat. It usually wore off fairly quickly. Secondly, stainless steel barrels were usually marked "—STAINLESS STEEL—" rather than "—NICKEL STEEL—"

Stainless steel barrels were made from 1924 on (circa serial #938,000) in limited numbers. The type of stainless steel then available was deemed not suitable for rifle barrels and the experiment was discontinued. A stainless steel barrel on an M1892 does not increase its collector's value.

The Models of 1886 and 1892

Barrel Bands
Front Barrel Bands
The front barrel band on the M1892 carbine is similar in appearance to the *M1873* Type 2 front barrel band but they are not interchangeable. The M1892 front and rear barrel bands were, however, identical to and interchangeable with the front and rear barrel bands used on the *M1894* carbine.

The front barrel band was installed only on the .38 and .44 caliber M1892 carbines. The magazine tube for the .25 and .32 caliber carbines was secured in place by the same magazine tube ring used on rifles. See Figure 5-54.

The front barrel band was 7/16 inches long, 1 27/64 inches high, 5/64 inches thick and milled to the shape of a figure "8." The top loop for the barrel was 39/64 inches in diameter and the bottom loop for the magazine tube was 41/64 inches in diameter.

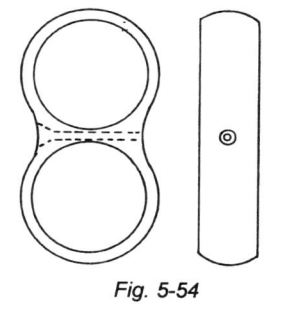

Fig. 5-54

A hole was drilled on either side of the front barrel band for the front barrel band screw. On the left, the hole was 1/8 inches in diameter and countersunk to 13/64 inches in diameter. The hole on the right side was 7/64 inches in diameter and was threaded 4-56. It was not countersunk.

Rear Barrel Bands
Two types of rear barrel bands were used on the M1892 Carbine. The **Type 1** rear barrel band was installed from the start of production to circa serial #900,000. It had internal shoulders and was 1 3/64 inches wide at its widest point, below the shoulders. It was 27/64 inches long by 1 3/4 inches high and milled from steel stock 5/64 inches thick. The top arch for the barrel was 1 21/64 inches high and 43/64 inches wide from shoulder to shoulder. See Figure 5-55.

Winchester Lever Action Repeaters

The rear barrel band had holes centered on either side. The left side hole was 9/64 inches in diameter and counter sunk to 7/32 inches in diameter for the rear barrel band screw. The right side hole was 7/64 inches in diameter and threaded 4-56. It was not countersunk.

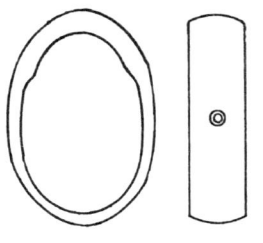

Fig. 5-55

The **Type 2** rear barrel band was used from circa serial #900,000 to the end of production. It was made of stamped steel 5/64 inches thick. It lacked internal shoulders but was formed with exterior shoulders that followed the contour of the barrel and forearm. See Figure 5-56.

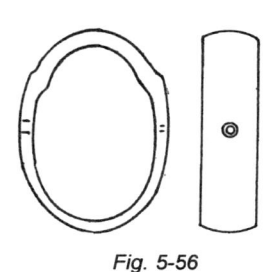

The Type 2 rear barrel band was 13/32 inches long and 1 23/32 inches high. The entire loop was 1 23/32 inches high, 3/4 inches wide at the shoulders and 13/16 inches wide at its widest point. The screw holes dimensions and thread were the same as the Type 1 barrel band. The Type 2 rear barrel band did not fit the forearm and barrel as snugly as did the Type 1, often leaving a slight gap.

Fig. 5-56

Barrel Band Screws

The barrel band screws were inserted from the left side. The front barrel band screw was 23/32 inches long. Its beveled head was 13/64 inches in diameter and 5/64 inches high. The shank was 41/64 inches long and threaded 4-56 for 5/32 inches. It was interchangeable with the front barrel band screws used on the M1894 carbine. See Figure 5-57.

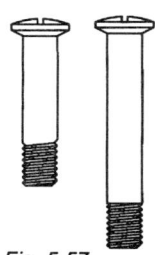

Fig. 5-57

The rear barrel band screw was 1 7/32 inches long. It had a beveled head 13/64 inches in diameter and 3/32 inches high. The shank

The Models of 1886 and 1892

was 1 3/64 inches long and threaded 4-56 for only 13/64 inches. It was interchangeable with the rear barrel band screw used on the M1894 carbine.

Front Sling Eye

The front sling eye was usually installed on the bottom of the rifle forend tip or the bottom of the rear barrel band on carbines. When no rear sling eye was installed on the carbine buttstock, the sling was fastened to the front sling eye and to the carbine's saddle ring.

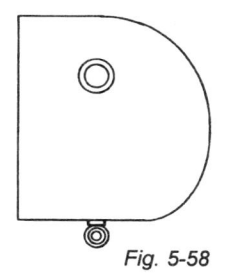

The front sling eye, see Figure 5-58, was 7/16 to 1 1/2 inches long *after* installation, depending on exactly which of several types were installed. The eye itself had a 23/64 inch outside diameter and a 13/64 inch inner diameter. The flange was 5/16 inches in diameter and 1/32 inches high. The hole was countersunk on both sides to 19/64 inches in diameter.

Fig. 5-58

The front sling eye stud was 1/2 to 9/16 long *before* installation. It was inserted into the rifle's forend tip or the carbine's rear barrel band through a 9/64 inch diameter drilled hole. The hole was not counterbored or counter sunk. The protruding end of the stud was crushed to retain the sling eye in place. See Figure 5-59.

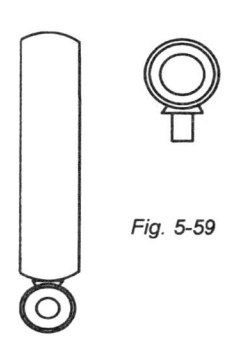

Fig. 5-59

Rarely, the front sling eye was retained by a washer and pin arrangement. As this required an extra manufacturing step, it was seldom used unless specifically requested. It was also sometimes installed with the washer, but without the pin or pinhole. Finally, the hole for the sling hook was centered and not offset to the top as in the rear screw eye.

Winchester Lever Action Repeaters

Magazine Tubes

Magazine tubes for rifles and carbines were identical in all respects save length and diameter. Two diameters of magazine tubes were manufactured. Those installed on the .25 and .32 caliber rifles and carbines had an outside diameter of 17/32 inches and the inside diameter was 15/32 inches. Those installed on the .38 and .44 caliber rifles and carbines had an outside diameter of 41/64 inches and the inside diameter of 37/64 inches.

Two types of the magazine tubes were made: the **Type 1** magazine tube had one hole 7/32 inches in diameter drilled for the magazine tube end plug screw 5/32 from the front edge of the tube to the center of the hole.

The **Type 2** magazine tube had two holes. The outer hole on the underside of the tube was 7/32 inches in diameter to accommodate the head of the magazine tube end plug screw and located 5/32 inches from the end of the tube to the center of the hole. The second, or interior hole, was 5/32 inches in diameter and located 11/64 from the front edge of the magazine tube.

Both types of magazine tubes were made of 1/32 inch thick steel sheeting rolled around a mandrel. A seam ran the length of the magazine tube where the edges joined. This edge was always turned to face the underside of the barrel.

NOTE: Reproduction magazine tubes are almost always extruded and do not have seams.

When the magazine tube end plug screw was properly installed, the front barrel band on carbines could be put on or taken off without having to remove the magazine end plug screw and thus releasing the magazine tube spring.

The Models of 1886 and 1892

Rifles with full length magazine tubes installed almost always used the long end plug screw that penetrated both surfaces of the tube and the width of the magazine tube end plug. An unthreaded portion of the shank protruded through the magazine tube and into a shallow hole in the bottom of the barrel to hold the tube in place against recoil.

Large caliber rifles used the end plug with lip and the *long* screw as did some late carbines—those with the ramp front sight and barrel band behind the sight. In this case, the distance from the muzzle to the magazine retainer seems to have dictated which screw was used.

A few rifles with full length magazines used the magazine end plug with a lip that rotated into a slot in the underside of the barrel. Short screws were usually used with this type of magazine end plug.

NOTE: The question of what magazine end plug was installed on a particular rifle or carbine is complicated by the fact that whenever an assembler felt the magazine tube was too loose, he installed the magazine end plug with lip.

Nearly all carbines used the magazine tube end plug that was held in place by a short screw. The magazine tube was secured against recoil by the front and rear barrel band screws on the .38 and .44 caliber carbines or the magazine tube ring pin and the rear barrel band screw on the .25 and .32 caliber carbines.

Magazine capacity for the standard rifle was fourteen cartridges and eleven for the carbine, regardless of caliber, with a proper length magazine tube spring. (See page 175)

The M1892 magazine tube was interchangeable with those of certain other models as shown in Table 5-9, below. The M1892 .38/.44 magazine tube was the same diameter inside and out as the M1866 and M1873 in .38 and .44 caliber but was not threaded for the screw-in

Winchester Lever Action Repeaters

end plug as found on the early M1866 and M1873s. Replacing the threaded tube with the unthreaded tube will require changing the end plug and will be incorrect for its period of manufacture.

TABLE 5-9
MODEL 1892 MAGAZINE TUBE
INTERCHANGEABILITY

MODEL 1892 CALIBER/SIZE	MODEL 1866	MODEL 1873	MODEL 1894
.25/.32 O.D. 17/32 I.D. 15/32		.32 caliber	
.38/.44 O.D. 41/64 I.D. 37/64	.44 caliber Those not threaded for screw-in magazine plug	.38/.44 caliber Those not threaded for screw-in magazine plug	All calibers

Magazine Tube End Plugs

Eleven different magazine plugs were used on the M1892 rifle and carbine. They are described in Table 5-10, below.

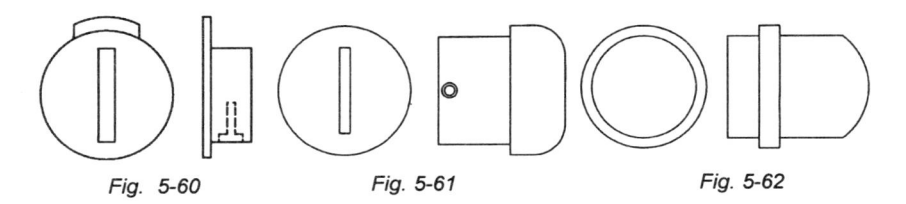

Fig. 5-60   Fig. 5-61   Fig. 5-62

All magazine Tube End Plugs were held in place by either the long or the short screw with the exception of Types 10 and 11 which were secured only by the forend tip. All magazine tube end plugs except for Types 10 and 11 were drilled with a hole 1/8 inch in diameter. The head end was counterbored to 13/64 inches in diameter to allow the screw to sit far enough down that its head was flush with the magazine tube's outer surface when properly installed.

The Models of 1886 and 1892

TABLE 5-10
MODEL 1892 MAGAZINE TUBE END PLUGS

Type	Cal.	Dia.	Profile	Slot	Lip Height	Lip Width	Screw	Note
1	.38/.44	9/16	Flat	Y	3/64	5/16	Short	1. See Fig 5-60
2	.25/.32	29/64	Flat	Y	3/64	17/64	Short	1
3	.38/.44	9/16	Flat	Y			Long	2
4	.25/.32	29/64	Flat	Y			Long	2
5	.38/.44	9/16	Flat	Y			Short	3
6	.38/.44	9/16	Round	Y	3/64	5/16	Short	4. See Fig. 5-61
7	.25/.32	29/64	Round	Y	3/64	17/64	Short	4
8	.38/.44	9/16	Round	Y			Long	4
9	.25/.32	29/64	Round	Y			Long	4
10	.38/.44	9/16	Round	N			No	Flange (5) See Fig. 5-62
11	.25/.32	29/64	Round	N			No	Flange (5)

1. Prevalent on late production rifles; 2. Most often used on rifles; 3. Most often used on carbines; 4. Used with fractional length magazines; 5. Use caution when removing the forend cap holding the Type 10 and 11 magazine tube end plug in place. There are no screws to secure it and the tension of the magazine spring will drive it forward with sufficient force to cause injury.

173

Winchester Lever Action Repeaters

NOTE: If the magazine tube end plug screw must be removed to allow the front barrel band on the .38 and .44 caliber carbines to be removed, either the screw is incorrect or not installed properly or the magazine end plug is incorrect. Marlin magazine end plugs will fit Winchester magazine tubes but the screw threads are not the same and they lack the screwdriver slot and thus will not fit properly.

Magazine Follower
The magazine follower was a short tube closed at one end, made of tubular steel. Two types of magazine tube followers were used. The magazine follower had a flange which butted against a corresponding flange in the magazine tube opening to prevent the follower from entering the action after the last cartridge. See Figure 5-63.

The **Type 1** magazine follower for the .25/.32 caliber rifles and carbines was 27/64 inches in diameter and 23/32 inches long. Its flange was 29/64 inches in diameter and 3/16 inches long. It was identical to the magazine follower used in the .32 caliber Model 1873.

The **Type 2** magazine follower was used with the .38/.44 caliber rifles and carbines. It was 17/32 inches in diameter and 31/32 inches long. Its flange was 35/64 inches in diameter by 1/2 inches long. It is identical to, and interchangeable with the magazine follower in the Model 1894.

Magazine End Plug Screws
Two types of magazine end plug screws were used. The **Type 1** magazine screw (short) was 9/32 inches long overall. It had a head 13/64 inches in diameter and 1/16 inches high. The shank was 1/8 inches in diameter and its entire length was threaded 6-48. See Figure 5-64.

Fig. 5-63

The Type 1 short screw penetrated only one wall of the magazine tube and screwed into the magazine end plug. The screw hole was counterbored so that the head was flush with the magazine tube surface.

The Models of 1886 and 1892

The **Type 2** magazine screw (long) was 25/32 inches long overall. It's head was 13/64 inches in diameter by 1/16 inch high. The shank was 1/8 inches in diameter and threaded 6-48 for only 7/32 of an inch at the *head end* only. The tip of the shank was beveled to facilitate easy penetration into the hole in the bottom of the barrel. See Figure 5-65.

The Type 2 long screw penetrated both sides of the magazine tube and the magazine end plug. The threaded head end screwed down into the counterbored recess so that the head was flush with the magazine tube surface. The end of the screw projected beyond the magazine tube wall and into a recess drilled in the bottom of the barrel to help hold the magazine tube in place against recoil.

Fig. 5-64

Magazine Tube Spring

The magazine tube springs used in the M1892 Winchester were made of spring steel wire. Two types were used.

The **Type 1** magazine tube spring was used with the .25/.32 caliber magazines. It had a diameter of 23/64 inches. It was identical to the magazine tube spring used in the M1873 .32 caliber rifle and carbine. The rifle spring has approximately 107 coils and should extend 6 inches beyond the end of the magazine tube. The carbine spring has approximately 86 coils and will extend approximately 4 inches beyond the magazine tube.

The **Type 2** magazine tube spring was used with the .38/.44 caliber magazines. It had a diameter of 7/16 inches. It was identical to the magazine tube spring used in the Henry, M1866, M1873 in .38 and .44 calibers and all M1894 rifles and carbines. The rifle spring has approximately 95 coils and should extend 6 inches beyond the end of the magazine tube. The carbine spring has approximately 75 coils and will extend approximately 4 inches beyond the magazine tube.

Winchester Lever Action Repeaters

Magazine Tube Rings

Four types of magazine tube rings were used with the M1892. All were made from 3/64 inch thick steel tubing. See Figure 5-66.

The magazine tube ring slot on standard rifles and on carbines of .25/.32 caliber was an elliptically-milled cutout in the bottom of the barrel, 3 25/32 ± 1/16 inches behind the muzzle to the front edge of the slot.

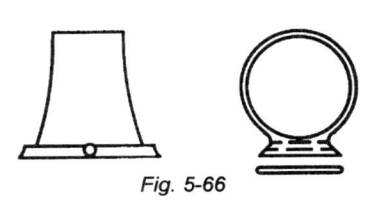

Fig. 5-66

On takedown variations, the magazine tube ring slot was located anywhere between 3 to 3 1/2 inches behind the muzzle to the front edge of the slot.

The **Type 1** magazine tube ring was used with .25/.32 caliber magazine tubes. It had an outer diameter of 5/8 inches and an inner diameter of 17/32 inches. Its base was 29/64 inches wide by 53/64 inches long and 5/64 inches high. A 5/64 inch diameter pin hole was drilled through the base from side to side for the magazine ring pin. It is identical to the magazine tube ring used on the M1873 .32 caliber rifle and carbines. This pin hole was drilled slightly above the bottom of the base. The pin did not "penetrate" the magazine tube but passed through a shallow groove cut across the diameter of the tube.

The **Type 2** magazine tube ring was used with the .25/.32 caliber takedown rifle. It had an outer diameter of 5/8 inches and an inner diameter of 17/32 inches. Its base was 29/64 inches wide by 53/64 inches long and 5/64 inches high. It did not have a hole drilled for the magazine ring pin.

The Type 2 magazine tube ring was also installed as a second ring to secure the magazine tube on any .25/.32 caliber rifle with a barrel longer than 30 inches.

The Models of 1886 and 1892

The **Type 3** magazine tube ring had an outer diameter of 47/64 inches and an inner diameter of 21/32 inches. Its base was 7/16-31/64 inches wide by 53/64 inches long and 5/64 inches high. A 5/64 inch diameter pin hole was drilled through the base from side to side. It was used on all standard .38/.44 caliber rifles.

This Type 3 magazine tube ring was also used on the M1866 and M1873 in .38 and .44 caliber and on all M1894 rifles.

The **Type 4** magazine tube ring was used on the takedown rifles in .38/.44 caliber. It had an outer diameter of 47/64 inches and an inner diameter of 21/32 inches. Its base was 7/16-31/64 inches wide by 53/64 inches long and 5/64 inches high. It did not have a hole drilled for the magazine ring pin.

The Type 4 magazine tube ring was also installed as a second ring to secure the magazine tube on any .38/.44 caliber rifle with a barrel longer than 30 inches.

NOTE: Twenty-six magazine tube ring bases were measured. The .38/.44 magazine tube rings exhibited a variance of between 7/16 and 31/64 inches in width while no measurable variance was found in the width of the .25/.32 magazine tube rings.

Two different pins were used. Both pins used with the Type 1 and Type 3 magazine tube rings were 5/64 inches in diameter. The .25/.32 caliber pin was 29/64 inches long . The .38/.44 caliber pin was 33/64 inches long. The .25/.32 caliber pin was the same as that used to hold the M1873 .32 caliber magazine tube in place. The .38/.44 caliber pin was also used to hold the M1866 and M1873 magazines in .38/.44 caliber in place, as well as all M1894 magazines of whatever caliber.

Winchester Lever Action Repeaters

Sights
Rifle Rear Sight
The standard rear sight for the M1892 rifle was the sporting rear sight. Before 1904 (circa serial #254,000) the notched elevator lacked a thumbpiece (see Figure 5-67); after 1904 the elevator was made with a serrated thumbpiece (see Figure 5-68). The two types were installed simultaneously to the end of production.

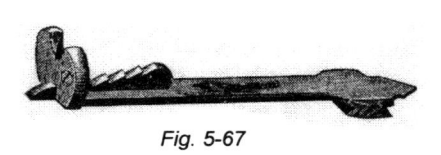

Fig. 5-67

The sporting rear sight was furnished with either a flat top (see Figure 5-69) or with a semi-buckhorn (see Figure 5-70). It was 3 1/32 ± 1/32 inches long overall and 21/32 ± 1/64 inches wide at the base where it slid into the rear sight dovetail cut into the barrel. The height for the sighting device at the rear was 31/64 ± 1/64 inches. The cutout for the rear sight elevator was 7/64 inches wide by 5/8 to 13/16 inches long. The variations in dimensions result from the amount of polishing the sight was subjected to before finishing.

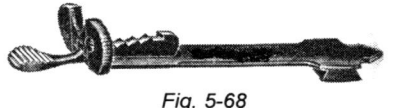

Fig. 5-68

Both the flat top and semi-buckhorn rear sights were furnished in two variations, with and without an adjustable blade or leaf. The leaf could be raised or lowered by means of a small screw. The adjustable blade was rarely furnished except on late guns or on special orders because of the cost of its manufacture. The adjustable blade had a "V" notch on the upper side and a square notch on the lower side. Either could be used simply by removing the screw and turning the blade upside down.

Fig. 5-69

The Models of 1886 and 1892

NOTE: The length of the elevation slide cutout is not important, but the **width** is. Marlin firearms were equipped with semi-buckhorn rear sights similar to the Winchester design but with elevation slide cutouts 5/64 inches wide. Both Winchester and Marlin rear sight dovetails were 3/8 inches wide. Measure the elevation slide cutout carefully to distinguish the two types.

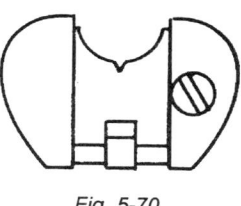

Fig. 5-70

Three variations of rear sight elevators were installed on the M1892 rifle with the semi-buckhorn sight.

Variation 1 was a straight-walled elevator without a thumbpiece, 1 3/32 long by 3/32 inches wide. It had six adjustment steps from 0 to 250 yards in 50 yard increments. It was used almost exclusively from the start of production to circa serial #250,000. It was unmarked. Refer to Figure 5-67.

Variation 2 was 1 21/32 inches long by 3/32 inches wide. It had a serrated, almost flat thumbpiece at the rear, 1/4 inches wide and 25/64 inches long and was oval shaped to aid in adjusting the elevation. It had six steps from 0 to 250 yards in 50 yard increments. The thumbpiece had seven grooves or serrations milled diagonally. It was unmarked and rarely installed, and then only after circa serial #250,000. Refer to Figure 5-68

Variation 3 was also installed intermittently with the two previous variations from circa serial #250,000 to the end of production. It was identical to Variation 2 except that it was marked with the patent date on the left side. The marking was 21/32 inches long and in block letters without serifs 1/16 inch high and read:
PAT.FEB.5.1901.
There was no spacing between words or numbers and periods were used rather than commas. The line always ended with a period.

Winchester Lever Action Repeaters

Carbine Rear Sight
The standard rear sight for the M1892 carbine was the ladder-style rear sight which Winchester referred to as the Sporting Leaf Sight. It was used until very late in production when the sporting rear sight with the flat top or semi-buckhorn sight was installed in conjunction with the ramp front sight. See Figure 5-71.

The sight base was 1 15/16 ± 1/32 inches long and the base at the dovetail was 23/32 ± 1/32 inches wide. The ladder was 1 23/32 ± 1/32 inches long.

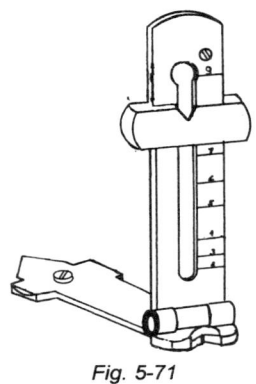

Two variations of the sight were installed. Nominally, those installed on the .38/.44 caliber carbines had a leaf graduated from "0 to 9," similar in style to those used on the M1873 carbine leaf sight. For carbines in .25/.32 caliber, the leaf was marked in gradations from "0 to 20."

Fig. 5-71

NOTE: The author has observed a great many .38/.44 caliber carbines with the Sporting Leaf Sight graduated from "0 to 20," that he was convinced were installed at the factory. He does not feel that the graduations of the sight leaf should affect overall value.

Front Sights
Rifle Front Sight
The standard front sight installed on the rifle was either a steel base with a milled silver, brass, nickel or steel blade. If a steel blade was used, the blade was molded as one piece into the base. If silver, nickel or brass, the blade was press-fitted into slot cut into the base. The sides of the sight blade tapered outward slightly near the base. See Figure 5-72.

Silver blades predominated while brass, steel or nickel blades were rare. They were 5/8 ± 1/64 inches wide by 11/32 inches long.

The Models of 1886 and 1892

The base was 3/8 inches long by 5/8 inches wide and milled from steel. It was slotted into a dovetail milled into the barrel 3/8 inches long, 51/64 ± 1/32 inches behind the muzzle to the start of the sight dovetail cut. This measurement can often be used to determine if a rifle barrel has been cut down.

Throughout most of M1892 rifle production, the front sight base was adjustable. A small screw penetrated the base on the right side. The base was locked in place by the screw which could be loosened to move the entire sight side-to-side to make minute adjustments in windage. Because the dovetail fit tightly and a great deal of force was needed to make the adjustment after the screw was loosened, the screw was often not installed at the factory, or was omitted by the owner at a later date. The presence or absence of the screw has no bearing on the collectors value of a M1892 rifle so equipped unless the sight base has a threaded hole from which the screw is missing.

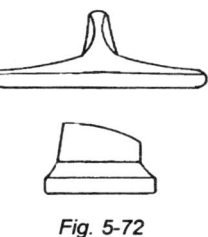

Fig. 5-72

The front sight screw was 9/64 inches long overall. It did not have a head. The screw was threaded 6-48 along its entire length.

Carbine Front Sight

Two types of front sights were installed on the M1892 carbine. Both styles were silver-soldered, or "sweated" onto the barrel.

The **Type 1** carbine front sight was a steel post with an integral blade 19/64 ± 1/64 inches wide by 11/32 ± 1/64 inches long by 21/64 inches high installed from the start of production to circa serial #250,000. It was located on the top surface of the barrel 1 3/64 ± 1/32 inches behind the muzzle. This measurement can be used to determine if a barrel has been cut. See Figure 5-73.

Winchester Lever Action Repeaters

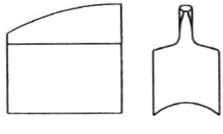

Fig. 5-73

The **Type 2** carbine front sight (Figure 5-74) was used from circa serial #250,000 to the end of production. It was also a steel post soldered to the top of the barrel, but a separate blade was pinned into a slot. The blade was made of steel, nickel, silver, ivory or any combination of these materials.

The post for the Type 2 carbine front sight was 9/32 ± 1/64 inches wide by 11/32 ± 1/64 inches long by 7/32 ± 1/64 inches high. The pin which secured the blade was 1/16 inches in diameter by 17/64 inches long.

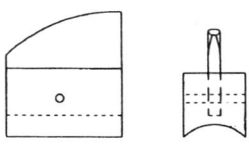

Fig. 5-74

The Type 2 front sight was located on the top surface of the barrel 1 3/64 ± 1/32 inches behind the muzzle. This measurement can be used to determine if a barrel has been cut.

Special Order Sights

Special order sights were available but were rarely ordered. Special order sights seldom result in a significant increase in value in the M1892 except in the case of tang sights or side-mounted receiver sights.

NOTE: If a factory letter indicates that special order sights were installed on a M1892 rifle or carbine and they have been removed, the collector's value of the rifle or carbine will be reduced by at least the cost of restoring the missing sights with originals. This is particularly true of all Winchester Lever Actions on which the factory-installed side receiver sight is missing.

Tang Sight

The most common special order sight on the M1892 was the tang sight. It was similar to the tang sight mounted on the M1894 but will almost always be coded differently. The code is found on the under side of the base. If manufactured by Lyman, the code will read "W", "D", "B", or "D.A". If manufactured by Marble Arms, the code will read "W1" or "W2". See Figure 5-75.

The Models of 1886 and 1892

The tang sight base was 2 11/16 inches long. The mounting screw holes were spaced 2 3/16 inches apart, center to center. The post on the M1892 tang sight was mounted 13/16 to 7/8 inches behind the front edge of the base to the center of the post.

Side-Mounted Receiver Rear Sight
Side-mounted receiver sights were made in a variety of configurations and sizes and are quite confusing. Any side-mounted receiver sight manufactured for the M1892 rifle or carbine can be determined by the fact that, no matter how it is coded on the inside surface of the mounting bar, it will be 3 5/16 inches long from the center of the "front mount" or "pivot screw" to the center of the "rear" or "pointer screw." See Figure 5-76.

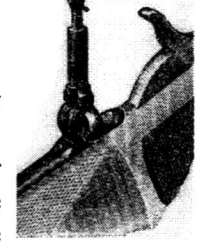

Fig. 5-75

Those side-mounted receiver sights manufactured by Lyman for the M1892 will usually be coded on the inside surface of the mounting bar, "D", "DA" or "DB". They will interchange with the M1894 side-mounted receiver sights with the same codes.

Fig. 5-76

NOTE: The code found on the inside of the mounting bar on side-mounted receiver sights vary too widely to be used to determine originality. Only the measurement given above, and a factory letter from the Cody Firearms Museum (see Appendix H) will prove original factory installation. Winchester records are surprisingly complete in this regard.

M1892 Screw Types and Sizes
Screws for the M1892 that were common to more than one model Winchester are shown in Table 5-11. The thread sizes for all M1892 screws are shown in Table 5-12.

183

Winchester Lever Action Repeaters

TABLE 5-11
MODEL 1892 SCREWS
COMMON TO MORE THAN ONE MODEL

Buttplate screw	1866 (late), 1873, 1876, 1886, 1894, 1895
Carrier screw	1894
Forearm tip screw	1866, 1873, 1876, 1886, 1894
Finger lever pin stop screw	1894
Front band screw, carbine	1894
Rear band screw, carbine	1894
Hammer screw	1894 is the same but slightly longer
Loading gate (spring cover) screw	1866, 1873, 1876, 1894
Magazine end plug screw, short	1866, 1873, 1876, 1886, 1894
Magazine end plug screw, long .25/.32 cal.	1873, .32 cal.
Magazine end plug screw, long .38/.44 cal.	1873 .38/.44 cal., 1894 all calibers
Mainspring screw	1894
Mainspring strain screw	1894
Rear sight lock screw, ladder sight	1866, 1873, 1876, 1886, 1894
Rear sight slide retaining screw, ladder sight	1866, 1873, 1876, 1886, 1894
Tang screw (stock bolt)	1866 (late), 1873, 1894, 1895
Tang sight mount hole plug screw	1866 (late), 1873, 1876, 1886, 1894, 1895 (if drilled and tapped- quite rare)
Trigger spring screw	1866, 1886

The Models of 1886 and 1892

TABLE 5-12
MODEL 1892 SCREW THREAD SIZES

SCREW	THREAD
Carrier screw	3/16-36
Cartridge guide screw	6-48
Front sight screw	6-48
Forend tip screw	6-48
Finger lever pin stop screw	11-36
Front band screw, carbine	4-56
Hammer screw	3/16-36
Locking bolt pin stop screw	6-48
Magazine lever screw, takedown	6-48
Magazine end plug screw, long	6-48
Magazine end plug screw, short	6-48
Mainspring screw	9-32
Mainspring strain screw	9-32
Rear band screw, carbine	4-56
Loading gate (spring cover) screw	6-48
Tang sight mount hole plug screw	3/16-36
Tang screw (stock bolt)	12-28
Trigger spring screw	3/16-36

Appendix A

MODEL 1886 SERIAL NUMBERS	
YEAR	NUMBER AT YEAR'S END
1886	1 to 3,211
1887	14,728
1888	28,577
1889	38,401
1890	49,723
1891	63,601
1892	73,816
1893	83,261
1894	94,543
1895	103,708
1896	109,670
1897	113,997
1898	119,192
1899	120,571
1900	122,834
1901	125,630
1902	128,942
1903	132,213
1904	135,524
1905	138,838

Year	Serial
1906	142,249
1907	145,119
1908	147,322
1909	148,237
1910	150,129
1911	151,622
1912	152,943
1913	152,947
1914	153,859
1915	154,452
1916	154,979
1917	155,387
1918	156,219
1919	156,930
1920	158,716
1921	159,108
1922	159,337
No further serial numbers were recorded until the M1886 was discontinued in 1935 at 159,994	

Winchester Repeating Lever Action series serial numbers supplied courtesy of U.S. Repeating Arms Company, New Haven, CT

Appendix B

\	M1892 SERIAL NUMBERS
YEAR	NUMBER AT CALENDAR YEAR'S END
1892	1-23,701
1893	35,987
1894	73,508
1895	106,721
1896	144,935
1897	159,312
1898	165,431
1899	171,820
1900	183,411
1901	191,787
1902	208,871
1903	253,935
1904	278,546
1905	315,425
1906	376,496
1907	437,919
1908	476,540
1909	522,162
1910	586,996

1911	643,483
1912	694,752
1913	742,675
1914	771,444
1915	804,622
1916	830,031
1917	853,819
1918	870,942
1919	903,649
1920	906,754
1921	910,476
1922	917,300
1923	926,329
1924	938,641
1925	954,997
1926	973,896
1927	990,883
1928	996,517
1929	999,238
1930	999,730
1931	1,000,727
1932	1,001,324

Winchester Repeating Lever Action series serial numbers supplied courtesy of U.S. Repeating Arms Company, New Haven, CT

Appendix C

Model 1886 Special Order Barrels

Few subjects are as confusing as the matter of special order barrels for the M1886 rifle. The following points should help the collector to identify "correct guns" as produced by the Winchester factory, and eliminate fakes.

Heavy and Extra Heavy Barrels
The principal difference between the variations of the M1886 configured with the "heavy" and the "extra heavy" barrels and the standard variations was the width of the flats on octagonal barrels and the overall diameter of the round barrels. These dimensional changes so altered certain parts that they were no longer interchangeable with parts from the standard rifles.
* The forend barrel channel and forend tip were cut wider to accommodate the additional width or diameter.
* The dovetails for both rear and front sights were wider but the sight base dimensions remained unchanged. When installed on both the heavy and extra heavy barrels, the sight bases will not completely fill the dovetails.
* The elliptical magazine tube cutout for the magazine tube ring was also cut wider. Winchester used the standard magazine tube rings as the magazine tube dimensions did not change, and they did not completely fill the cutout.
* The dovetail for the forend tip tenon located under the forearm tip was also cut wider and again, Winchester used the standard forend tip tenon and so they will not fill the cut.
* Winchester milled and threaded the breech ends of heavy and extra heavy barrels exactly as they did the standard barrels, so no alterations to the receiver were necessary.

Lightweight and Extra Lightweight Barrels
Winchester produced the Model 1886 "lightweight" and "extra" lightweight variations in .33 and .45-70 calibers, *only*. Any other caliber rifle, albeit one configured identically in every respect, was considered by Winchester to be a "special order" rifle.
    The primary difference between the lightweight and Extra Lightweight special order rifles and the standard rifles is the width of their "rapid taper" barrels. This meant that certain dovetails and other assemblies attached to the barrel differed from the standard configuration.
* The forend was narrower and thinner, making it more fragile than

the standard forearm, and subject to cracking and splitting with even a moderate blow.

* The forend tip tenon was considerably shorter from side-to-side as the forend tip was made thinner to fit the barrel. The tenon will not interchange with the standard tenon but will interchange with that used on the continuation Model 71.

* The front and rear sights applied to the lightweight and extra lightweight barrels were the same as used on the standard rifles. Both will overflow their dovetails even though the front sight was mounted in a raised ramp soldered to the top of the barrel.

* Magazine tube rings installed on lightweight and extra lightweight barrels had narrower bases and will fit their slots without overflowing. The magazine tube rings for the lightweight and extra lightweight barrels are the same length front to rear as standard magazine ring bases, but are narrower laterally, measuring 13/32 inches wide as compared to 31/64 inches wide for the standard magazine ring. You should exercise care with the narrow magazine ring base as it will slide out of its slot with little pressure on rapid taper barrels. The slot lips are very thin and are prone to damage easily.

* The forend tip tenons installed on lightweight and extra lightweight barrels are shorter laterally than the standard tenon to fit the narrower forend tip, and so they cannot be interchanged. They may interchange with the narrower forend tip used on the continuation Model 71, however.

* The forend tip used on the lightweight and extra lightweight barrels were 1 3/64 inches long overall and 1 3/32 inches wide, making it narrower than the standard rifle forend tip. The magazine tube hole also was a complete circle (these barrels were made only in the round configuration) unlike the standard forend tip which has a 7/32 inch opening at the top. The magazine tube opening on forend tips for the M1886 was unique at 49/64 inches diameter, no matter which barrel was installed, and so serves as a point of identification. Refer to Figure 4-56.

* Both the lightweight and extra lightweight variations of the M1886 had stocks with overly large and deep "lightening" cuts hollowed out, rapid tapper, 22 or 24 inch barrels, thinner than standard forearms and forearm tips with narrower and shallower barrel channels, narrow magazine tube ring bases and forearm tip tenons noticeably narrower than the standard tenon.

* How do you tell the difference between lightweight and extra lightweight variations of the M1886? Examine the buttplates. The lightweight variations always had shotgun-type steel buttplates installed while the extra lightweight variations had shotgun type-hard rubber buttplates.

Appendix D

The Model 1886 .50 Caliber Rifle

The .50 caliber M1886s, rifles and carbines, were extensively modified and hand fitted to make them function reliably. Winchester parts lists did not differentiate between parts for the .50 calibers arms and parts for other calibers. Check all .50 caliber M1886s carefully. The following six characteristics define a .50 caliber Model 1886 rifle.

1) All .50 caliber chambers were polished at the top rear (lined area). This polishing often impinged upon the threads anywhere from "very slightly" to "almost through." Because the .50 caliber Winchester cartridge case was larger in diameter than other cartridges chambered for the M1886, there was very little rim support at the top of the chamber.

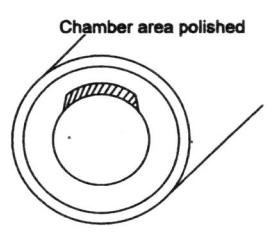

Chamber area polished

2) All .50 caliber cartridge carriers were milled out to receive the larger diameter .50 caliber cartridge case. If a .50 caliber Winchester case does not rest in the carrier snugly, it is not a .50 caliber carrier.

3) All cartridge guides were milled 20/1000 inches thinner than the standard cartridge guide. The metal was removed from the outside surface where it touches the inside surface of the receiver.

4) Finger levers used on .50 caliber M1886s were milled off just in front of the carrier hook to allow the loading gate to open far enough to admit the larger diameter .50 caliber cartridge case.

Hatch lines signify area milled away to permit loading gate to open further to receive wider .50 caliber cartridge case.

Finger lever modification for .50 W.C.F cartridges

5) All .50 caliber magazine tubes had a portion of the right hand rear (receiver end) surfaces milled to a knife edge.

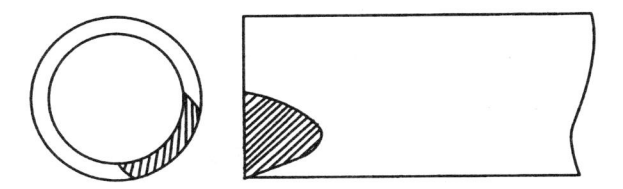

6) Some .50 caliber magazine ports were milled in an arc on the right side (arrow)

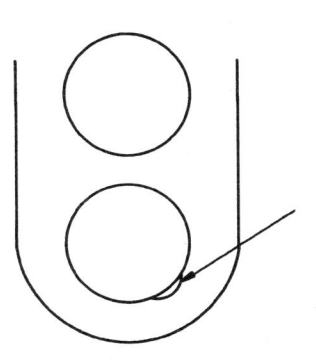

Appendix E

Winchester Ammunition for the Model 1886

Cartridge	AKA	Bullet Weight (Grains)	Powder Charge (Grains)	Muzzle Velocity (FPS)	Year of Introduction
.45-70		300	70	1,300	1886
.45-70	.45-70 Government	405	70	1,350	1886
.45-70	.45-70 Government	500	70	1,315	1886
.45-70	.45-70 W.C.F.	330	70	1,300	1886
.45-70	.45-70 W.C.F.	350	70	1,320	1886
.45-90	.45-90 W.C.F.	300	90	1,530	1886
.40-82	.40-82 W.C.F.	260	82	1,490	1886
.40-65	.40-65 W.C.F.	260	65	1,420	1886
.38-56	.38-56 W.C.F.	255	56	1,395	1887
.50-110	.50 Express	300	110	1,600	1887
.40-70	.40-70 W.C.F.	330	70	1,383	1894

.38-70	.38-70 W.C.F.	255	70	1,490	1894
.50-100	.50-100-450 W.C.F.	450	100	1,475	1895
.45-85	.45-85 W.C.F. Express	300	85	1,554	1896
.45-85	.45-85 W.C.F. Express	350	85	1,510	1896
.33	.33 W.C.F.	200	41 grains of 3031	2,200	1903

Winchester Ammunition for the Model 1892

.44-40	.44 W.C.F.	200	40	1,310	1873
.38-40	.38-40 W.C.F.	180	40	1,330	1879
.32-20	.32-20 W.C.F.	80	20	2,100	1882
.32-20	.32-20 W.C.F.	100	20	1,290	1882
.25-20	.25-20 W.C.F.	86	20	1,460	1895
.218	.218 Bee	46	12	2,910	1939

Appendix F
Glossary

The words contained in the list are defined as they apply to Winchester Lever Action Repeating Firearms

Assembly Number	A unique number applied to a set of parts that have been fitted together to permit proper assembly into a finished firearm at a later time.
Baby Carbine	Any carbine with a shorter than standard (20 inch) barrel. Also known by the nickname, "trapper carbine."
Bluing	A chemical or heat process by which the top layers of steel or iron are oxidized to a blue-black color.
Bushing	A removable threaded sleeve which screws onto the face of the breechbolt in early M1866, 1873 and 1876 firearms to steady the firing pin.
Buttplate	A piece of metal, rubber or plastic shaped to cap the end of the buttstock.
Buttstock	The shoulder stock of a firearm.
Carbine	Short-barreled shoulder arm designed for use by horsemen. A carbine usually has a flatter buttplate than a rifle and some means of securing the firearm to the saddle to prevent loss.
Chamber Face	The rearmost portion of the barrel shank which can be observed by opening the breech and examining the chamber. It appears as a ring around the breech.
Case Harden	The process by which iron or steel is heated in the presence of carbon (bone meal or charcoal) then cooled quickly to form a wear-resistant layer of hard metal over a softer core. If the heated metal is cooled in water, characteristic mottled tones of blue, red and yellow are imparted to the metal. This is referred to as color case hardening. If the metal is cooled in oil, a dull black sheen is imparted.
Comb	The part of the buttstock on which the shooter's cheek rests.
Cradle	Area within the carrier block milled to fit the cartridge as it is forced from the magazine tube

	and lifted in the carrier block to the breech.
Crown	To machine the end of a barrel to produce a rounded end.
Dovetail	A slot cut wider at the bottom than at the top to facilitate mounting a sight or tenon on a barrel.
Dust Cover	Sliding cover mounted on top of the frame designed to prevent dust and dirt from entering the action and jamming it. See also Mortise Cover.
Extra Finish	Wood stocks, forearms or forends that showed "figure" or grain pattern greater than that supplied on standard stocks, forearms or forends.
Fillister Head	A machine screw with a rounded head and straight shoulders.
Flange	A rim or rib on a half magazine tube cap to hold it in place.
Flat Head	A machine screw with a flat head and shoulders angled inward to the shank. Also a wood screw.
Flats	The flat portion of an octagonal barrel.
Forearm	Wooden grip used on carbines.
Forend	Wooden grip used on rifles.
Grooves	The area between the lands in a bore.
Head	Refers to the top portion of a screw in which is usually cut a slot for a screwdriver.
Heel	The extreme upper rear portion of the buttstock.
Italic	*A type face characterized by being slanted to the right.*
Lands	The raised spirals inside a barrel which engrave the bullet and impart spin to increase accuracy.
Lip	A projection or edge such as that on certain of the magazine end caps which rotate into a groove in the barrel.
Loading Gate	Winchester's term was "Spring Cover."
Lower Tang	The lower rear projection of the receiver used to attach the buttstock and certain other action mechanisms.
Lower Tang Screw	A wood screw on the extreme rear of the lower tang which penetrates into the stock. It has the same thread as the buttplate screw but is slightly shorter.
Mortise Cover	Sliding cover mounted on top of the frame designed to prevent dust and dirt from entering

Oval Head	the action and jamming it. See also Dust Cover. A machine screw with a rounded head and shoulders angled inward to the shank. Also a wood screw.
Proud	Term applied to the wood raised above the metal around an inletted cut.
Receiver	The part of a firearm to which are attached the barrel, stock, finger lever and other actuating mechanisms.
Rifle	A Winchester Lever Action Repeating firearm with a barrel usually longer than 20 inches. The presence of a forend distinguishes a rifle from a carbine.
Round Head	A machine screw with a rounded head and no shoulders. Also a wood screw.
Safety Bar	See Safety Catch
Safety Catch	Mechanism that locks the trigger to prevent the firearm from discharging unless the action is completely closed. Winchester used this term but many modern collectors refer to it as the trigger or safety bar.
Screwdriver Slot	The straight cut made in the face of a magazine tube cap to facilitate removal from the tube.
Serial Number	Unique and usually sequential number or combination of numbers and letters applied to a firearm, originally for assembly and accounting purposes, and since 1968 in the United States of America, as a federally-mandated means of identification.
Serif	Short line or stroke projecting, usually at an angle, from the end of a letter.
Shank	Refers to the threaded end of the barrel which screws into the receiver. Also to the threaded end of a screw.
Short Rifle	A Winchester lever action repeater with a barrel length less than 24 inches. Twenty to 22 inches was standard for most short rifles; 22 inches for the M1876 short rifle.
Shoulder	The sides of a screw head or the sloping area between the neck and body of a cartridge case.
Special Order	A firearm ordered from the Winchester factory by a customer with specific accessories such as

	sights, barrel length and shape, figured wood, checkering or finish.
Spur	The projecting portion of the hammer which the thumb uses to cock or release the firing mechanism, or the tang at the top of some shotgun-type buttplates.
Standard	Refers to regular production rifles, carbines and muskets not subject to special order features such as engraving or extra-special wood.
Stirrup	The link between the hammer and mainspring.
Tenon	A machined piece of metal fitted into a dovetail slot in the underside of rifle barrels. The forend tip is held to the tenon by two screws.
Toe	The extreme lower rear portion of the buttstock.
"Trapper" Carbine	Collector's term applied to any lever action carbine with a barrel shorter than the standard 20 or 22 inches. Trappers were thought to want compact firearms that could be carried and used efficiently in the thick brush or marshes that lined river banks.
Trigger Bar	See Safety Catch.
Upper Tang	The upper rear projection of the receiver to which the buttstock is attached.
Upper Tang Screw	The screw or bolt that attaches the buttstock to the receiver by passing through both the receiver tang and the buttstock.
W.C.F.	Winchester Center Fire
Wrist	The part of the buttstock gripped by the hand when in proper firing position.
X, XX, XXX	Fancy, fancier, fanciest wood stocks, forearms and forends.

Appendix G

Bibliography

Angier, R.H., "Firearm Blueing and Browning," T.G. Samworth, 1936, Stackpole Company, Harrisburg, Pennsylvania.

Barnes, D., G.R. Watrous, J.C. Rikhoff, T.H. Hall and P. Kuhlhoff, "The History of Winchester Firearms, 1866-1980," 5th Edition, Winchester Press, 1980. ISBN 0-87691-324-9

"Catalogs of the Winchester Repeating Arms Company, 1865 to 1918," Reprinted by Armory Publications, Armory Publications, P.O. Box 4206 Oceanside, CA 92052-4206.

Flayderman, Norm, "Flayderman's Guide to Antique American Firearms . . . and their values," DBI Books, Inc., Northfield, Illinois, 6th edition, 1994. ISBN 0-87349-112-2

Madis, George, "The Winchester Book," Art and Reference House, Brownsboro, Texas 75756, 1961. ISBN 0-910156-03-4

Madis, George, "Winchester Dates of Manufacture," Art and Reference House, Brownsboro, Texas 75756, 1981.

Pardee, Bruno, U.S. Winchester Repeating Firearms Company, New Haven CT 06511, Private Communication regarding Winchester Lever Action serial numbers.

Parson, John E., "The First Winchester," Winchester Press, New York, 3rd Edition 1969.

Phillips, Roger F. and Donald J. Klancher, "Arms and Accoutrements of the Mounted Police 1873-1973," Museum Restoration Service, Bloomfield, Ontario, Canada, 1982 ISBN 0-919316-84-0

Phillips, Roger F., and S.J. Kirby, "Small Arms of the Mounted Police," Museum Restoration Service, Ottawa, Ontario 1965.

Pirkle, Arthur, "Winchester Lever Action Repeating Firearms, Volume 1, The Models of 1866, 1873 and 1876," North Cape Publications, Tustin, CA 92780, 1994.

Stone, George W., "The Winchester 1873 Handbook," Frontier Press, Arvada, Colorado, 1973.

Wilson, R.L., "Winchester, An American Legend," Random House, New York, 1991. ISBN 0-394-58536-4

Wilson, R. L., Winchester: The Golden Age Of American Gunmaking and the Winchester 1 of 1000," Buffalo Bill Historical Center, Cody, Wyoming, 1983. ISBN 0-931618-12-6

Appendix H

Cody Firearms Museum, Buffalo Bill Historical Center, Cody, Wyoming

The Cody Firearms Museum, located at the Buffalo Bill Historical Center, P.O. Box 1000, Cody, Wyoming 82414 (307 587-4771), is the repository not only for the original Winchester factory collection of firearms but surviving Winchester factory records (also Marlin and L.C. Smith). Many of these records list the type, caliber, style of barrel, type of trigger, type and style of furnishings, finish and date of shipment for many, but not all, Winchester-produced arms. The cost to obtain a letter describing a particular firearm is currently $40.00 each for two letters in one year, $35.00 each for up to four letters, $25.00 each for up to nine letters and $20.00 each for ten or more. Your letter is sent on special Cody Firearms Museum letterhead and is signed by the Curator.

The Cody Firearms Museum operates a membership program as well. Annual fees begin at $150.00. Members are entitled to 40 free record searches by telephone (up to four serial numbers at one time), Monday through Friday during normal working hours and a reduced rate of $25.00 per letter for one to five letters in any one year, $20.00 for six to nine letters and $15.00 for ten or more letters. Members receive other benefits as well, concerning the museum itself.

To obtain a letter regarding a particular Winchester firearm (or Marlin or L.C.Smith), address your letter to the Curator at the above address. Supply the name of the manufacturer, model number and serial number of the firearm in question and enclose a check for the proper amount.

About the Author

Arthur K. Pirkle was born in Augusta, Georgia and raised in the Smokey Mountains of western North Carolina near Burnsville. He joined the Marine Corps after High School and served two tours of duty in South Vietnam. He is now a retired Marine Corps Master Sergeant and a novelist as well as a thirty-year-plus collector of, and dealer in, Winchesters and Colts. He is an Endowment Member of the National Rifle Association and lives in Yuma, Arizona with his wife of forty years, Patty.

THE MOSIN-NAGANT RIFLE

OTHER BOOKS FROM NORTH CAPE PUBLICATIONS®, INC.
The books in the "For Collectors Only" and "A Shooter's and Collector's Guide" series are designed to provide the firearm's collector with an accurate record of the markings, dimensions and finish found on an original firearm as it was shipped from the factory. As changes to any and all parts are listed by serial number range, the collector can quickly assess not only whether or not the overall firearm is correct as issued, but whether or not each and every part is original for the period of the particular firearm's production. "For Collectors Only" and "A Shooter's and Collector's Guide" books make each collector and shooter an "expert."

For Collectors Only Series

The .45-70 Springfield, Revised, 3rd Edition, by Joe Poyer and Craig Riesch ($16.95) covers the entire range of .45 caliber "trapdoor" Springfield arms, the gun that really won the west. "Virtually a mini-encyclopedia . . . this reference piece is a must." Phil Spangenberger, *Guns & Ammo*

U.S. Winchester Trench and Riot Guns and other U.S. Combat Shotguns by Joe Poyer ($15.95). Describes the elusive and little-known "Trench Shotgun" and all other combat shotguns used by U.S. military forces. "U.S. military models 97 and 12 Trench and Riot Guns, their parts, markings [and] dimensions [are examined] in great detail . . . a basic source of information for collectors." C.R. Suydam, *Gun Report*

The M1 Carbine: Wartime Production, Revised, 3rd Edition, by Craig Riesch ($16.95) describes the four models of M1 Carbines from all ten manufacturers. Complete with codes for every part by serial number range. "The format makes it extremely easy to use. The book is a handy reference for beginning or experienced collectors." Bruce Canfield, Author of "M1 Garand and M1 Carbine"

THE MOSIN-NAGANT RIFLE

The M1 Garand 1936 to 1957, Revised 2nd Edition, by Joe Poyer and Craig Riesch ($19.95). "The book covers such important identification factors as manufacturer's markings, proof marks, final acceptance cartouches stampings, heat treatment lot numbers . . . there are detailed breakdowns of . . . every part . . . in minute detail. This 216 page . . . volume is easy to read and full of identification tables, parts diagrams and other crucial graphics that aid in determining the originality of your M1 and/or its component parts." Phil Spangenberger, *Guns and Ammo*

Winchester Lever Action Repeating Firearms, by Arthur Pirkle.
Volume 1, **The Models of 1866, 1873 & 1876** ($19.95)
Volume 2, **The Models of 1886 and 1892** ($19.95)
Volume 3, **The Models of 1894 and 1895** ($19.95)
These famous lever action repeaters are completely analyzed part-by-part by serial number range in this first new book on these fine weapons in twenty years. ". . . book is truly for the serious collector . . . Mr. Pirkle's scholarship is excellent and his presentation of the information . . . is to be commended." H.G.H., *Man at Arms*

The SKS Carbine, Revised 2nd Edition, by Steve Kehaya and Joe Poyer ($16.95). The "SKS Carbine" is profusely illustrated, articulately researched and covers all aspects of its development as well as . . . other combat guns used by the USSR and other Communist bloc nations. Each component . . . from stock to bayonet lug, or lack thereof, is covered along with maintenance procedures . . . because of Kehaya's and Poyer's book, I have become the leading expert in West Texas on [the SKS]. Glen Voorhees, Jr., *Gun Week*

British Enfield Rifles, by Charles R. Stratton
Volume 1, **SMLE (No. 1) Mk I and Mk III** ($16.95)
"Stratton . . . does an admirable job of . . . making sense of . . . a seemingly hopeless array of marks and models and markings and apparently endless varieties of configurations and conversions . . . this

THE MOSIN-NAGANT RIFLE

is a book that any collector of SMLE rifles will want on his shelf." Alan Petrillo, *The Enfield Collector's Digest*

Volume 2, The Lee-Enfield No. 4 and No. 5 Rifles ($16.95) In Volume 2, "Skip" Stratton provides a concise but extremely thorough analysis of the famed British World War II rifle, the No. 4 Enfield, and the No. 5 Rifle, better known as the "Jungle Carbine." It's all here, markings, codes, parts, manufacturers and history of development and use.

Volume 3, The Enfield Magazine Rifles (and their Conversions) will be published at a later date.

Volume 4, The Pattern 1914 and U.S. Model 1917 Rifles ($16.95). This volume provides a history of the development and use of the Pattern 1914 rifle by the British during World War I and its adoption and by the U.S. military in .30-06 caliber. More Model 1917 Enfields were produced between 1917 and 1919 by Winchester, Remington and Eddystone than Model 1903 rifles at Springfield Armory. Sgt. Alvin York captured half a regiment of German soldiers with a M1917 Enfield. All the markings, codes, parts and manufacturers are listed and described from the collector's point of view for both the British and American versions.

The Mosin-Nagant Rifle, Revised, 2nd Edition, by Terence W. Lapin ($19.95). For some reason, in the more than 100 years that the Mosin-Nagant rifle has been in service around the world, not a single book has been written in English about this fine rifle. Now, just as interest in the Mosin-Nagant is exploding, Terence W. Lapin has written a comprehensive volume that covers all aspects and models from the Imperial Russian rifles to the Finnish, American, Polish, Chinese, Romanian and North Korean variations. His books set a standard that future authors will find very difficult to best.

THE MOSIN-NAGANT RIFLE

The Swedish Mauser Rifle by Steve Kehaya and Joe Poyer ($19.95). The Swedish Mauser rifle is perhaps the finest of all military rifles manufactured in the late 19th and early 20th Centuries. A complete history of the development and use of the Swedish Mauser rifles is provided as well as a part-by-part description of each part. All 24 models are described and a complete description of the sniper rifles is included. All markings, codes, regimental and other military markings are charted and explained. A thorough and concise explanation of the Swedish Mauser rifle, both civilian and military.

A Shooter's and Collector's Guide Series

The M16/AR15 Rifle, by Joe Poyer ($19.95.). The M16 has been in service longer than any other military rifle in the history of the United States military. Its civilian counterpart, the AR15, has recently replaced the M14 as the national match service rifle. This 134 page, profusely illustrated, large format book examines the development, history and current and future use of the M16/AR15. It describes in detail all civilian AR15 rifles from more than a dozen different manufacturers and takes the reader step-by-step through the process of accurizing the AR15 into an extremely accurate target rifle. Ammunition, both military and civilian is discussed and detailed assembly/ disassembly and troubleshooting instructions are included.

M14-Type Rifles, A Shooter's and Collector's Guide, Revised, 2nd Edition, by Joe Poyer ($14.95). A study of the U.S. Army's last and shortest-lived .30 caliber battle rifle which became a popular military sniper and civilian high power match rifle. A detailed look at the National Match M14 rifle, the M21 sniper rifle and the currently-available civilian semiautomatic match rifles, receivers, parts and accessories, including the Chinese M14s. A guide to custom-building a service type-rifle or a match grade, precision rifle. Includes a list of manufacturers and parts suppliers, plus the BATF regulations for building a "banned" rifle look-alike.

THE MOSIN-NAGANT RIFLE

The SAFN-49 Battle Rifle, A Shooter's and Collector's Guide, by Joe Poyer ($14.95). The SAFN-49, the predecessor of the Free World's battle rifle, the FAL, has long been neglected by arms historians and writers, but not by collectors. Developed in the 1930s at the same time as the M1 Garand and the SVT38/40, the SAFN-49 did not reach production because of the Nazi invasion of Belgium until after World War II. This study of the SAFN-49 provides a part-by-part examination of the four calibers in which the rifle was made. Also, a thorough discussion of the SAFN-49 Sniper Rifle plus maintenance, assembly/ disassembly, accurizing, restoration and shooting. A new exploded view and section view are included.

Collector's Guide to Military Uniforms

The "Collector's Guide to Military Uniforms" endeavors to do for the military uniform collector what the "For Collectors Only" series does for the firearms collector. Books in this series are carefully researched using original sources and are heavily illustrated with line drawings and photographs, both period and contemporary to provide a clear picture of development and use. Where uniforms and accouterments have been reproduced, comparisons between original and reproduction pieces are included so that the collector and historian can differentiate the two.

Campaign Clothing: Field Uniforms of the Indian War Army
  Volume 1, 1866 to 1871 ($12.95)
  Volume 2, 1872 to 1886 ($14.95)
Lee A. Rutledge has produced a unique perspective on the uniforms of the Army of the United States during the late Indian War period following the Civil War. He discusses what the soldier really wore when on campaign. No white hats and yellow bandanas here.

A Guide Book to U.S. Army Dress Helmets 1872-1904, by Mark Kasal and Don Moore ($16.95).

THE MOSIN-NAGANT RIFLE

From 1872 to 1904, the men and officers of the U.S. Army wore a fancy, plumed or spiked helmet on all dress occasions. As ubiquitous as they were in the late 19th Century, they are extremely scarce today. Kasal and Moore have written a step-by-step, part-by-part analysis of both the Model 1872 and 1881 dress helmets and their history and use. Profusely illustrated with black and white and color photographs of actual helmets.

All of the above books can be obtained directly from North Cape Publications®, Inc, P.O. Box 1027, Tustin, CA 92781 or by calling Toll Free 1-800 745-9714. Orders only to the toll free number please. For information, call 714 832-3621. Orders may also be placed by FAX (714 832-5302) or via Email to ncape@pacbell.net. CA residents add 7.75% sales tax. Postage is currently $2.95 for 1-2 books, $3.75 for 3-4 books, $5.95 for 5-8 books. Priority Mail is $4.50for 1 book, $4.95 for 2-3 books. Write, phone, fax or Email for rates on larger quantities, or for international orders.

Also, visit our Internet web site at **http://www.northcapepubs.com**. Our complete, up-to-date book list can always be found there. Also check out our linked On-Line Magazine for the latest in firearms-related, magazine-quality articles and excerpts from our books.